PERMAFROST IS AN ARCHIVE

North
Alaska
Canada
Hwy
Mt.
Churchill

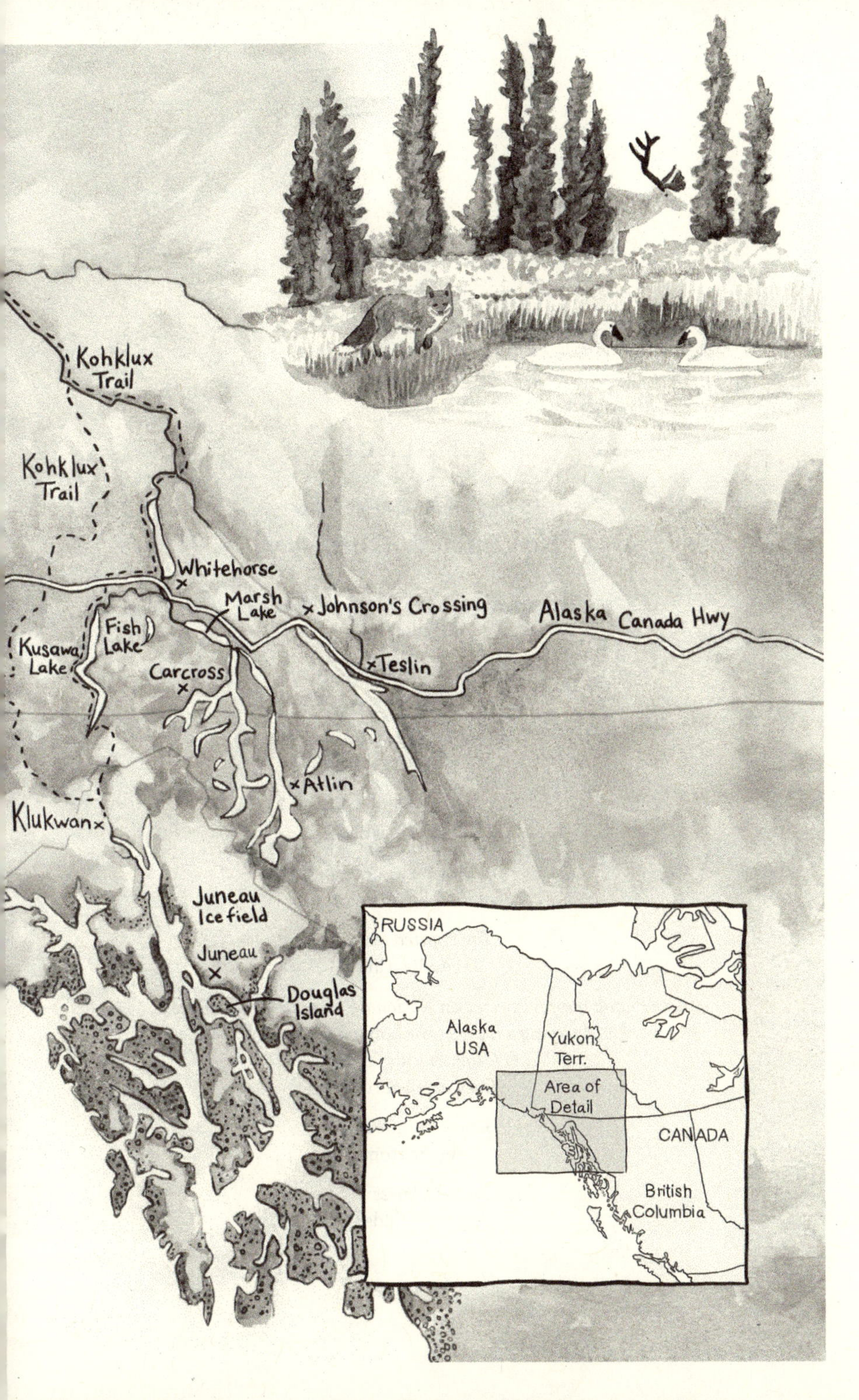
Kohklux Trail
Kohklux Trail
Whitehorse
Marsh Lake
Johnson's Crossing
Alaska Canada Hwy
Fish Lake
Kusawa Lake
Carcross
Teslin
Atlin
Klukwan
Juneau Icefield
Juneau
Douglas Island
RUSSIA
Alaska USA
Yukon Terr.
Area of Detail
CANADA
British Columbia

IN PLACE

Jeremy Jones, Series Editor
Elena Passarello, Series Editor

Clear Creek: Toward a Natural Philosophy
Erik Reece

Curing Season: Artifacts
Kristine Langley Mahler

A Year without Months
Charles Dodd White

American Vaudeville
Geoffrey Hilsabeck

This Way Back
Joanna Eleftheriou

The Painted Forest
Krista Eastman

Far Flung: Improvisations on National Parks, Driving to Russia, Not Marrying a Ranger, the Language of Heartbreak, and Other Natural Disasters
Cassandra Kircher

Lowest White Boy
Greg Bottoms

On Homesickness: A Plea
Jesse Donaldson

PERMAFROST IS AN ARCHIVE

and Other Inheritances from the Alaska-Yukon Borderlands

Corinna Cook

West Virginia University Press | Morgantown

First edition published 2026 by West Virginia University Press
Printed in the United States of America
ISBN 978-1-959000-70-9 (paperback) / ISBN 978-1-959000-71-6 (ebook) / 978-1-959000-85-3 (PDF)

Library of Congress Control Number: 2025032651

Cover design by Michel Vrana
Map by Kristin Link
Book design by Ashley Muehlbauer / AM Book Design
Image of Kohklux map (1869) courtesy of The Bancroft Library.

CONTENTS

PERMAFROST IS AN ARCHIVE

THE PHOTOGRAPHER (A PRELUDE)

The man bends over the earth, camera pressed to his face. He photographs rocks.

No. He does not photograph rocks; he photographs time. The man bends over the earth with one eye screwed shut while the other eye strains to see.

No. The man bends over the earth to feel its curvature. He holds a camera to his face so that the added weight will make his head bend with the light. He photographs neither rocks nor time; he photographs memory.

No, the man bends over the earth until one day his head falls off, drops over the edge of the horizon. The old cartographers were right. Beyond all the known edges lie the Greek monsters, or the Norse chasm of fire and ice. The photographer's head drops off beyond all known edges, plummeting toward one lucid thought.

Or perhaps the man bends over the earth and hears the voice of a child.

"Excuse me, sir. What are you photographing?"

If Antoine de Saint-Exupéry's character the Little Prince landed in Canada's eastern Arctic, say, Baffin or Ellesmere Island (rather than in the Sahara Desert as Saint-Exupéry places him), I am certain he would have met this photographer rather than a stranded pilot. And I am certain the Little Prince would have skipped introductions with the photographer just as he did with the pilot. I am certain the Little Prince would have said exactly these words: "Excuse me, sir. What are you photographing?"

The man who bends over the earth with a camera pressed to his face replies, "Rocks."

"Why are you photographing rocks?" asks the child.

"Because my camera can only snap an instant," says the man with the camera. "But the rocks hold eons. I am trying to get at them."

"At the eons?"

"At the eons."

"What do you want with the eons?"

The child, if he is the Little Prince, will persist in his questioning. The man with the camera may ask what a child is doing alone out in the mountains or the plains or the beaches of Ellesmere or Baffin Island, but the child will ignore the question. "What do you want with the eons?" If he is the Little Prince, he will repeat his question until he gets an answer.

The man with the camera tries to remember. He comes from distracted people—from an entire distracted civilization. But underneath, it is on the cusp of recalling something. At least the man with the camera is persuaded that this is the case: that he is about to remember something. That they are all about to remember something. That memory could break the surface any generation now. Any moment, even!

"What do you want with the eons?"

The Little Prince interrupts the photographer's thoughts, and the thinking photographer does not know what to say to the child.

But he knows how to bend over the earth. How to press a camera to his face. The island, be it Baffin or Ellesmere, is made of so many rocks he's sure to find time in those rocks, and he's sure to find memory in that time. So he bends over the earth, presses a camera to his face. He bends over the earth, screws one eye shut while the other strains to see. He bends so far he feels the earth's curvature. He bends like the light, which has been here all along, and that is when his head falls off, tumbling over the edge of the map.

The man's shoulders remain hunched, his hands cupping and adjusting the camera out over the void, snapping shot after shot, focusing, reframing, shooting, and focusing again.

"Perfect, perfect!" he mutters.

Photographers are people who thirst for the right light, you know. And they'll go to the ends of the earth to find it.

PART ONE

The Slower Questions

THE BLACK SPRUCE

To understand the black spruce, remember it grows from a fist-sized root ball as gray and compact and crucial as a brain. Each black spruce spindles itself straight up into the crack of the cold, stout branches making a skyward scrub from base to apex all winter night. And below that brain of roots lies permafrost, even in summer. This, then, is a tree that keeps ice in mind.

I remember meeting the black spruce years ago, during my first move from Southeast Alaska up to the interior. I was ill at the time, a fjordlands creature with an immune system gone haywire, taking temporary leave from the rainforest and from the whole glaciated coast against which my fevers flared. I would return to another region of this same inland, boreal biome a decade later, but back then, I aimed for semi-arid, boreal-forested Fairbanks. I hoped to find a kind of medicine.

It was end-summer, fall-not-winter when I went. The road north took me through Yukon and then across the Alaska border toward Tok. Here is what I remember: I rolled down the highway and the spruce flanking the road shot me an uncanny glance. Thus arrested, I glanced back.

Hello

Said the black spruce

We are the toughest things you have ever met.

Those black spruce on the road to Tok, they told me something about where I was going and what kind of cure I might find. They said it straight—with their tight skyward shape, their dark color, their dry firm trunk-stems as spindly as old canes, their flaking skin bark and waxy stout needles, that fierce clod of roots that looks like a dry brain—they said just what it means to live outside. In winter. And to do it well.

As if falling into step with a tree might heal my ailment.

I reeled a little bit. I was still sick, see—strong enough to drive, but not strong enough to open my car door in a crosswind.

Yet I heard them clearly.

Hello

Said the black spruce

We are the toughest things you have ever met.

I learned something about myself then: If the trees will talk, I will listen.

What did I hear? For starters, those trees' toughness so far exceeded mine that I laughed out loud.

We are the toughest things you have ever met, they repeated, *except maybe for chickadees.*

Deadpan truth-humor. The black spruce appreciated my laughter. That is how I became friends with a kind of a tree.

I thought of Emily Dickinson, of course—

I'm Nobody! Who are you?

Are you – Nobody – too?

So it went that on land that loves to be frozen—that lives for it, really—I sidled up to a kind of tree, the black spruce, the tree that keeps ice in mind. I paused in Fairbanks for a few years to consider this. A pair of nobodies before those all-important chickadees, the black spruce and I leaned in shoulder to shoulder; we went on arm in arm.

■ ■ ■

Some years later and many miles south, my mother gives me the gift of a painting. An artist from Juneau, Constance Baltuck, has returned from a residency with the Parks Service. A crew of some sort brought her into the backcountry of the Kobuk Valley for a few weeks. The crew did their science—counting caribou?—while Constance set up her easel every day. Made sketches. Then she returned home, some eight hundred miles southeast of the Kobuk, completed a series of paintings, and had a show. My mother picked a painting from this show.

It's the trees, my mother explains. *It's not the flashiest painting of Constance's Kobuk series*, but there is *something about the trees*. The trees remind her of when I took my leave of our rainforested island and passed those seasons in Fairbanks. She figures the painting will remind me, too.

It's an arctic summer landscape. The greenery in the foreground is lush and streaked with yellows and dotted with pinks and oranges; an urgent bloom. There is one cluster of five black spruce standing together; otherwise they are in twos and ones—this is not a forest landscape, but perhaps the northernmost reach of black spruce habitat. The far plane of hills is abstracted to dusk colors, gray lavender mauves, and the sky behind is clouded, pale gray-blues shaded in the shape of cumulous billows. High clouds, puffy, but dense. Summer sky bearing down hard on land that just holds its breath, waiting for a good hard frost to clear the air.

■ ■ ■

In Fairbanks's Goldstream Valley, where I first got to know the boreal forest, the black spruce grow in the low places, wetlands or bogs, while birch trees grow on hills where the ground is drier. But soil type is only one of the differences between birch and spruce habitat. There are also inversions. During winter's coldest spells, an inversion sends the most bitter air downhill into the bogs while a fluff of warmer air sits on top. Above the inversion among the birches, it may be twenty below—but forty below beneath the inversion among the black spruce.

I wintered both ways. And as it had by the side of the sea, my immune system kept its own counsel: Persistent reactions came and went. Sometimes they swelled, ruptured the skin, and became the site of strange infections. For one winter I nursed these while living in a cabin among the birch trees above the inversion. And for two winters I pondered these flare-ups from a home below the inversion, alongside the black spruce.

Have it either way on the question of "warm" and "cold." Two Rivers poet Derick Burleson cuts to the chase by gauging not winter's cold but winter's color. He arrives at an understanding of blue, sees in the winter night the birch trees glow blue, sees their shadows cast dense blues on the paler blues of the snowpack. Derick sees even the blue shadow of his breath. But that breath itself—this makes a cloud of white rolling out into the air over blue snow, against blue tree trunks in a birch stand. I reread his book *Melt* to verify all this. Indeed, the moon, the snow, the birch—all the hues of winter are blue save one: There is white in the poet's exhaled breath alone.

I was grateful to Derick for teaching my eye to see how shades of blue bind the snow and the moon and the birch trees and everyone's night shadows to winter, to cold.

And so imagine my surprise when one night I perceived red.

It was there among the black spruce, down in the deepest night cold. Unmistakable. A one-color aphorism inscribed in the trees. I adjusted, centered my attention, and proceeded to study those trees long and hard for many months, for many looping miles. I studied that red by touch and by tongue. I studied by sorrow, by insistence. I found heat. And I didn't know what to make of it, for with the ebb and flow of my own fevers this much was clear: My illness was at its core also a kind of heat. Yet the black spruce, spindling their heat up into the crack of winter cold, were fine.

About the black spruce in Constance's painting: They are flecked with red. They are flecked with flaming red paint.

I am awash when I see the painting and tell my mother over and over to look at the red. *Those trees* are *full of red!* I say. *They are!*

Are they? she asks me, pleased, an interested gardener. She hasn't spotted any red in real spruce herself; then again, she lives on Alaska's southeast coast, not in black spruce habitat. But like many mothers, she knows me better than should be possible. She picked me a painting and she picked this one because she thought it might touch on my inland life, hook something, reel it forth.

Are black spruce really full of red? she still asks now and again, pleased, not particularly concerned about how literally or metaphorically I mean it.

Yes! I say.

Yes: I say it over, and over. There is, I'm sure, something the boreal forest reveals about the larger, slower questions. Something a neighbor's dashing red flecks reveal about the future.

▪ ▪ ▪

Looking back, I don't know that I found a kind of medicine during those subarctic winters. I do know that I grew quite close to a kind of tree, the black spruce, and that I missed them when I left. I also know the experience feels unfinished (imbalanced), as if the black spruce gave me a gift of something elegant that I am too clumsy to properly wear. I try, for their sake, to consider red as a serious proposition—though it is not clear what this really demands.

And so I turn to memory and think back to those winters. How the snow came each October and I skied through the frozen bogs every day to the end of April. I skied by headlamp, by moonlight, by the scrape of sun sending its brief, midday lance across the earth. Especially during an inversion. If it was too cold to breathe or blink or budge, I skied. I think now that I did it specifically to be with the black spruce, over and over, three years in a row. To hear them thinking through the coldest of it, to gather what I could of how well they fared.

That is probably how I began to see beneath the surface of things. Through all the blue of snow and shadows I saw in the black spruce something red hot, something I might now describe as red hot ease with winter, red hot ease with lunar cold, its airless clamp.

What I'm saying is: It is easy to be a black spruce out in forty below. They really are flecked with red.

Though memory reminds me that when I first perceived their ease, again I just laughed. Copying them would be impossible. In my sick, strong, fragile, eager, confused animal body, it would be impossible to live as perfectly as a tree. This was as freeing a realization as any other, an echo of Franz Kafka: There is hope but not for us.

■ ■ ■

Still, I think of red.

Red, the heat of fire.

In the body, heat can occur at a cellular level. In excess, it is inflammation.

Medical science ties inflammation to aging. We might infer that aging (cellularly understood) is a condition of increasing inflammation.

But remember: Elders carry knowledge the young cannot fathom.

This strikes me as significant. Thus, what links inflammation to wisdom? What do I mean if I say, "The red heat of the wise"?

Although I don't know it at the time, in ten years or so I'll return inland. I'll plunk down in Whitehorse, Yukon, turning to another corner of the boreal forest for new counsel about different ailments entirely—the melting land, society's divisions on uncertain footing, the simple facts of interdependence and conflict. Again, I will want a better line of sight on the deep strangeness at hand. I always do. And I will always remember that when winter went airless with cold, I saw flecks of red in the strong and twisted spruce. Simply put, I glimpsed an uncanny answer to illness—mine or maybe a larger one—and that is a koan I now carry.

■ ■ ■

I see Constance at a dinner party somewhere in south Douglas. West Juneau maybe. I am so eager to talk to her about the red in those black spruce. I am brimming.

That red, that red—I don't know exactly what I say. Surely worry breaks the surface of me and I have to ask, *Do you remember you did that—you put red paint in with the black spruce?* Of course she does. Of course she remembers flecking those trees with red.

Perhaps we talk about her seeing what I see and the happy convergence of our seeings. Perhaps we talk about thinking in colors, joining concept to sight, question to hue. Or about perceiving truths just below the skin of the day. I'm not sure anymore. I do not really remember the conversation. Constance has curly, gray hair and a splashing smile. Her voice is small and we both let things like the exuberance of dinner parties wash our words out to sea.

■ ■ ■

Those flecks of red? I'll tell you what they are. Those flecks of red are a method. It is how a black spruce handles its heat, using it to live well winter upon winter upon winter. It is how a black spruce looks a person in the eye in order to say, *This is how to live in step with good, hard cold.*

Can a human body mimic the thinking of a tree? I try, I try.

■ ■ ■

The chickadees, though—they're something else. Singing this and that at the birdfeeder in forty below. Somehow this is possible: with their teeny black stick-legs and their teeny feathered bodies, somehow it is not only possible for chickadees to live through the winter night; it is also possible for them to chitter and flit, gamble and grouse, wheel and bicker and proclaim sudden notions. The black spruce and I, we watch in wonder, but have yet to find medicine in verbs like these. So we follow no chickadee's line of flight. We simply hold our admiration close where it grows, one neuron at a time, until we can make an idea of it, an idea with a mind of its own, which we quickly knob into the earth and guard until it grows thick as blood, bright as conviction, healthy as nightfall.

DISTANCE OVER LIGHT

POINT OF ORIGIN: DOUGLAS ISLAND, ALASKA

As a child I ached for open ocean. Too young, I wanted to pull the water all day with a paddle, feel the push of water on the hull of a kayak. When finally I was five and permitted out on protected waters, floating things called to me—a feather, a chip of ice. I'd reach out to touch those small perfections, afloat and temporary like me. I'd tap them once to see just how they rode on the surface of depths. But still I ached for open ocean, and when finally I was big enough to take my own kayak into the swell, nothing healed. That ache went down into the pit of me, made a home there.

Now grown, I ache most for bare rock: high ridges that know the bellies of clouds. Then, as now, I buckle for spare, clear places. Ones lying outside the edge of densities.

■ ■ ■

ORIENTING

The tear-shaped island in Alaska on which I grew up has steep, rainforested mountainsides. It has sharp, rocky shores. And it has a two-lane bridge to the mainland, where the rest of town is a capital city busy with state politics. Town is rimmed by fifteen hundred square miles of high-mountain ice; no road links our community to any other community. And so we take care of each other. We respect certain risks and not others. *The mountain doesn't know you're an expert*, we tell one another, because anything can turn. Any mistake can turn fatal, but so can no mistake at all. Conversely, mistakes can also skate, causing no harm and leaving only a what-if. And so life in our steep, sharp, cold home must, by necessity, be alert. And, by necessity, humble. For it's the rest of us, all the neighbors, who bear the brunt of responsibility for any misfortunes that befall another.

That is why child-me learned how to follow a watershed off the mountain to the beach. Without landmarks where the forest is thick, or when the weather is socked in with snow and rain, or if it is the time of year when darkness falls—child-me learned the points of reference that lead to tide line. My family taught me this early on because the rainforest is dense, but along the shoreline rescuers can concentrate a search. Now grown, I see self-rescue—or at minimum, stopping at nothing to make oneself findable—is only partially about personal safety. Most importantly, this is how we protect those on whom we depend.

In other words, I learned the first principle of respect for land and community is this: When I am lost—when, not if—there are exactly two options. Either I find myself. Or I make it possible for others to find me.

Still, I am often enough alone on a mountain these days. I am often enough alone with a line of sight on changing weather, a line of sight on a predator or signs of its passage, a line of sight on capricious terrain pulling me onward as if with hooks but promising no sure footing. I am responsible to those who would risk everything to come to my rescue. My physical location is always also an ethical one.

I buckle for spare, clear places, yes. Open water as a child, and now, bare rock: footpaths on stony ridges so narrow the French call them *arêtes*, indicating mountain spines thin as the bones of fish. But what do I make of the ease with which places like this could toss me away? As on the land and water, as in the widening circles of time.

■ ■ ■

HYPEROPIA (FARSIGHTEDNESS), A COMMON REFRACTIVE ERROR

Once, I left that tear-shaped island in Alaska and went to live in Missouri. I went to study literature, but found myself also daily compelled to study the Midwest. Regarding the former, I was well prepared. Regarding the latter, my points of reference didn't hold. And so my observations of Missouri were stilted, cartoonish: most days, I saw the place as largely paved. Paved, but upon closer inspection I found that between certain roads were farms, and between certain farms were patches of deciduous hardwood forest—in which I ultimately spent a good deal of time pondering Missouri's limestone bluffs, learning the names of wildflowers (spring ephemerals, they call them), and practicing hardwood tree identification.

I learned that North America's eastern hardwood forests stretched from the Atlantic all the way into the Midwest, dwindling only at Missouri's western edge. I learned that there, right along the westernmost margin of Missouri, the continent's vast expanse of hardwood trees gave way to the tallgrass prairie of the Great Plains. And I learned that when the earliest waves of colonial settlers reached Missouri's western edge—and thus the edge of the forest—American pioneers stopped moving west. They didn't know what to make of the Great Plains. Suspicious of that vast expanse, I imagine they crouched, peering out from under the limbs of the trees. They paused there for forty years. Almost two generations passed before pioneers mustered the courage to step out of the forest and into the plains, risking life in the open prairie. But they finally did. Around 1850 they moved into what's now Kansas, for example, joining and crowding the Plains Indians who had been living on the prairie all along.

"They moved," I wrote in the quick paragraph above. "Joining and crowding." Of course this picture is incomplete.

Accuracy would demand a fourth verb: "to massacre." And so I think about that. About how we carry our histories, how we carry the past we inherit, whether we know it or not.

But this essay is not a thorough retelling. This essay is a map of threads, strings pulled taut across the land. At best, this essay watches for the points at which its threads might bring each other into focus with disparate, conjoined lines of sight.

■ ■ ■

TRAVERSES (PART ONE): KANSAS, USA

The first time I left Missouri to cross southern Kansas, I went east to west on Highway 50, or perhaps Highway 54, and thought all day of the tallgrass prairie and the Plains Indians. Present-day agriculture somewhat eclipses both. Still, I tried to throw my mind underneath the industry at Kansas's surface. I thought of people who knew how to find their way on that wide land pressed right into the sky—people who knew how to find water, find animals, find their neighbors, find home. That is, all day I watched the land's flatness—dizzying—and thought of people who knew right where they were. All day I tried to understand where I was too; I tried to imagine finding my own way on the prairie. All day I failed. I was stumped in several dimensions at once. Stumped by the sheer scope of Kansas's industrial agriculture, stumped by the history of America's stupendous land grab, and stumped by the simple fact of flat topography, a shape I never learned to read in the steep sharp forests of the tear-shaped island in Alaska that I know best.

But the second time I set out to cross southern Kansas—west to east, this time—I realized the land is not flat. It tilts. The first clue: I found Kansas's air was thinner at its western edge. My own body told me that. First my lungs. Then, of course, my heart.

But it is not only the fact that Kansas tilts. It is the fact that from east to west Kansas tilts about the same distance into the sky as does the tear-shaped island in Alaska from which I come. More, even. More! I'm saying from tideline to the top of the peak, which the maps call "Bradley" and that we call "Jumbo," my mountainous, fjordlands island is like Kansas compressed and set on edge. I'm saying from the Flint Hills across the whole prairie, Kansas is like Douglas Island disguised as a table.

■ ■ ■

CIRCUMNAVIGATION

The fjordlands I come from lie along the northern edge of the Coast Mountains, a mountain range that delineates much of North America's western edge. Those mountains make a meteorological barrier: In the Coast Mountains' northernmost reaches, in my part of the world, west-facing peaks snag and anchor so many of the Pacific's roving cloud systems that the coastal side is carpeted with steep, temperate rainforest. Little precipitation ever reaches the mountain range's inland side, and there, the climate is semi-arid, continental. Home to the boreal forest and boreal forest dwellers.

At present the Great Plains are behind me. I've returned to the North where I'm spending one year inland, abroad, living among neighbors in Yukon, Canada. I'm watching four seasons wheel through the boreal forest, which flanks the other side of the mountain range. I'm here, of course, to think about how we northerners carry our histories. And about how we might shift and reshuffle the weight as we try to hold steady on melting land.

Recently, I met a Yukon-based landscape painter. Her subjects: Sea. Rock. Ice. Air. Her palette: grays and browns and every muted blue between. Her idea: refracted beams of bent light.

I see in her paintings something of the substance of my old ache. Perhaps its depth or its weight—perhaps simply the dimensionality of the open. The weight of clarity.

Some years ago the painter took a holiday to Norway and embarked on a sailing artist residency aboard a tall ship. She visited Svalbard on this wooden vessel with portholes below and skyward masts slung with cords and canvas sails above.

Aboard the tall ship and upon each of Svalbard's beaches where she stepped ashore, the painter worked with candles, sticks, and string. She sought a material way of thinking through old navigation techniques like triangulation and celestial observation, a material way of understanding her location in the physical world. *How*, the painter asked, *can the land tell us where we are? And where*, she asked, *do my own reference points split from others'?* We're all here together, after all. Yet we come from such different places, acting on such different convictions.

At sea, the painter created string prisms to mediate the line of sight dictated by the ship's portholes. On the beach, she set up strings aligned with distant landforms and, therefore, also aligned with history. She made lines and prisms and she pondered the old ways. This is how the painter watched, day after day, for the various points of reference—physical and imagined—by which different people through the ages found their way to Svalbard's shores.

I listen to the painter. And eventually I understand that tall ship as a restored history. Its technologies of the past ferry artists across the present, somehow going both into and away from the future. In this, the ship strikes me as a kind of map—as both a time and place to think about the paths leading to what we might call "here" and to what we might call "now."

■ ■ ■

CALCULATIONS

This spring, I make it a practice to sit alone on the floor of the Yukon Arts Centre, a spacious art gallery on the hill. I visit these Svalbard paintings, sprawl on the floor, one elbow stretched wide on the single wooden bench. Another clear, spare place, this well-swept gallery floor? Perhaps. A series of clear, spare places depicted in the painter's acrylics on canvas? Certainly. But more importantly, the painter's Svalbard series deals with optics: beams of light that interrupt my aching.

One painting, *I am Here*, is at a distance half brown and half gray: half land, half water and sky. Two perfections sharing one canvas. It is the result of close study. Candles, sticks, and string; geometric lines of sight across spare land yield this portrait of a wide open place full of air and cold light.

Clear—but cut by an optical idea, for three geometric beams come off three mountain slopes. Spare—but for the beams' convergence on the rocky beach, their convergence a small prism of pink dashed with tangerine, bright and small like a bud, an utterly impossible flash of light on ancient land.

My eye erases that small pink-orange prism. Perhaps because the prism is over-raw: a point on the canvas at which the underpainting reveals too much. Indeed, a typical underpainting is invisible. It is the first layer of color the artist puts down on the canvas, and it governs the tone of all the colors laid atop it. In this case, the underpainting is the foundation that inflects those grays, renders them as the exact grays they are. It is the base that determines the quality of those browns, creating the earth exactly as it is. In other words, the underpainting is not really for us to see, but it propels the image's life within.

And so my eye erases the prism, refuses to register its popping rose and tangerine portal to the canvas's deeper, primary layers.

But my aching mind circles that bright flash, circles and circles it. Yearning underlies my first thought, which is this: Light is just too quick to see. Light converges on surfaces in such a temporary, fleeting way.

And my second thought: Light—like life—converges on surfaces in such a temporary, fleeting way.

■ ■ ■

DECLINATION

During the fall I spend in Yukon, the berries just don't come. Grizzlies go hungry, don't den up when we expect them to; confusion and violence ensues. Later, strange midwinter thaws undermine the snowpack. Ultimately, snowcover is overthin all winter. It just doesn't build up. By spring, there's no runoff to water the land, which catches fire and burns for months. Everyone who breathes draws dense smoke into their lungs all day, and all night, for perhaps ten weeks. The world is changing. Even the air slips sideways. Beneath the smoke, salmon surge into the rivers where they have migrated annually for millennia, but countless go belly-up before spawning. We are accustomed to fish carcasses: The sea sends us this wealth every summer. But they ought to die after spawning, not before. We crouch on riverbanks, watching, pondering, then posting photographs of beached fish bellies, which dominate the digital gaze for weeks. The water, people say, is just too warm.

In other words, the world is both recognizable and not. So it is that we witness daily our epoch of transformation. So it is that we receive its complicated loss, over, and over, and over.

Still, there is this, true in the coastal place of my birth as in this inland place: Every day we must meet the steep, cold, sharp place in which we dwell with alertness, diligence, and humbleness, for every day the land surrounds us with concentrations of power and life. It must be this that leads young parents to teach a child how to follow a watershed to shoreline. It must be this that leads grade school teachers to design safety curricula alongside things like math and language arts. I still remember building shelters of moss and spruce boughs at Echo Cove in the late spring of sixth grade, as every sixth grader in the borough did then and perhaps still does. In any case, no one pretends the place is inert. It isn't. Nowhere is.

■ ■ ■

REFRACTIVE CORRECTIONS

Of Kansas's Flint Hills, native Missourian and Indigenous Osage writer William Least Heat-Moon writes: "The grasses allow me the illusion I can raise my arms to stir the bowl of heavens."

When I read this line, it is winter in Yukon. I may never see Missouri or Kansas again. But I picture Heat-Moon miles and miles out on the plains, arms raised, stirring the bowl of heavens, and I remember crossing Kansas myself. I remember the moment when I recognized in Kansas the same skyward reach of my tear-shaped island in Alaska. I remember throwing back my head with that realization. And now that I am reading Heat-Moon I can name that feeling. Recognizing Kansas felt like putting my mouth into the bowl of the sky.

Truly. And with recognition, Kansas opened toward me. I remember, I remember: Everything changed. An owl came while I walked the dog in the Flint Hills. With the owl, time eased up and slid like a drapery to the ground where I left it and took instead to the ease of walking. The rhythm made me strong and light and took me quite far and then farther still. And what of the ache? Was all this weightless ease a mark of my aching, or the antidote?

I don't know. But time, though I'd left it behind, somehow still passed—so that eventually it was later than it had been before, and I was driving again. That is when the tumbleweeds came. With two bounces on the windy road those tumbleweeds took all the rhythm and ease of my body and spread it over and into everything around; the dark soil, the bending grasses, even the wires of an inconsequential fence and the far, flat sky itself. They spring weightlessly as caribou, tumbleweeds do. Not bound to the earth's gravity at all. And yet essential in binding people to land and land to people.

That is what I mean when I say that Kansas opened toward me. My sense of ease suddenly and entirely surpassed the margins of my body, margins I thought were mine. So that something humming in me hummed all the more decisively around me.

The open, the open.

That is both how and when the mechanics set aside their farm machinery at six a.m. to repair my tire, and most crucially, that is both how and when the creased and wary men who take their coffee at the garage lit up, welcomed me in. They did this because although I had initially set out across Kansas to get somewhere else, they perceived—perhaps before I did—that I was not really passing through at all. I was there.

Perhaps it is sentimental, but it is also true. That cold spring morning in the open embrace of Kansas, I was brimming. And having told my story of owls and tumbleweeds to one of the creased and wary men who takes his coffee at the garage, he took me in, me and my shivering dog, and introduced me to the others like this. *She saw a hoot owl*, he said, and all of the quiet men who take their coffee in the garage took note. *Go on*, he prompted, *tell them how you saw a hoot owl*, and I did, I told them how the owl walked me outside of time and hurry and even discontent and that the tumbleweeds cracked everything open into the land itself. In turn, the creased men (who, I now realized, were not at all wary) spoke of clods of dirt and the roots that hold those clods. They remained quiet but they were eager, eager to show me more of the land, to speak for themselves of what I'd begun to glimpse. They spoke of the roots they'd looked at that morning, full of conviction and pride that the root was still good—still good under the frost—holding their crooked fingers up like hooked rootlets, feet strong and flat on the floor, eyes flashing, because that very morning they had yet again seen sheer strength cresting inside clods of the prairie's dark soil. They spoke and they gestured and light sprang from their eyes, and in this way, the men at the garage took me as kin.

Later, of all that knit us together in that early spring morning, I thought this: We are just people who listen to the land. We are just people who live every day with the ache of our listening.

Yes, I've left the Midwest since then. No, I have no home there. But I still see Kansas and Douglas Island as twinned and twinning places, two landmasses that rise the same three to four thousand feet into the sky—though Douglas rises that distance in less than six miles and Kansas in four hundred. Call it coincidental math, but for myself, I've come to believe a thicker kinship governs all this.

■ ■ ■

CONCURRENCES

Gray, in particular, captivates me. It is my favorite.

Tell me about your grays, I say to the painter, and that is how I learn that gray is no mix of black and white, but rather a mix of *color*—opposites on the color wheel that temper one another, draw one another to center. One comes to gray by a roundabout path, by mixing vibrant blue and orange, or the royalties of purple and gold. Blue draws the orange to center; orange draws blue to center. Purple draws gold closer to the sea; gold pulls purple sunward. They tone and temper and soothe and still one another. Vibrancies merge, approach stillness together, find a peace neither can make alone. Eventually, they balance. Eventually, perfection. Eventually, gray.

And your browns? I ask. *Of what is brown built?* Answers the painter: *One makes mud by mixing all the colors.*

I try to remember this, for it strikes me as essential.

All the colors—they make mud. That is the earth.

Two resplendent opposites—in joining, they grow still. They hold peace. That is gray.

Between the painting's gray half and its brown half lies only one incongruous detail, a narrow gold band. It crosses a small part of the rocky shore's clean browns, a waterside patch of strange brightness. I wonder if that gold is a glimpse of intertidal life. But I'll learn it's more complicated. That's the still-cycling nutritive tracing of an old history, a history of whale harvests and rendering their blubber, a golden haunting on the rocks.

I wonder, for a moment, if the artist listens to color so intently that she aches with the expanse of the whole light spectrum. I wonder if her heart bears a bruise from the weight of the color wheel resting on it.

■ ■ ■

CORPOREAL GEOLOGIES

Heat-Moon's book, the one I am reading this winter in Yukon, is called *PrairyErth*. Heat-Moon considers the book a "deep map" of a single county in the Flint Hills of Kansas because he's gathered Chase County's histories, geologies, politics, weather systems, cultures, mythologies, and economies, stitching them into the warp and weft of human voices.

Yet Chase County, Kansas is not Heat-Moon's home. Heat-Moon, a traveler and travel writer, a Missourian of English and Irish and Indigenous Osage heritage, roams the Flint Hills of Kansas as an outsider, a self-described woodlands dweller studying the prairie. He and his forest sensibility peer into the treeless plains, searching for lines of sight on America, expectation, invention. He and his forest sensibility triangulate, and triangulate, and triangulate, gathering points of reference into a constellation of well over six hundred pages. Spiritual cartography in prose.

To say *PrairyErth* is a deep map is to say *PrairyErth* is a map of aching.

I must tell you about one essay in particular. It reveals that an ancient mountain chain called the Nemaha Mountains underlies the Flint Hills of Kansas.

Once, I—a northern fjordlands creature—got my bearings in the flat heart of North America. It happened only once and it happened in Kansas. It happened when I recognized in Kansas's incremental tilt the same verticality I knew so well from the cliffs of the rainforested mountains that made me.

And Heat-Moon is here to say: Kansas has been sitting upon a great chain of mountains all along. The Nemaha Ridge.

When the Nemahas were uplifted on Pangea, they would have been as steep and striking as the Tetons. Eventually, the Nemaha Mountains were submerged into an ancient sea. Fifty million years of settling sediments covered them with strata upon strata of calcium carbonate, the stuff of which Kansas, as we now know it, is made. Of the four hundred oil wells in Chase County alone, only a handful go so deep as to scrape the highest ridges of those Precambrian mountains.

What lies below is core to understanding what sits above. I think of the Svalbard painting, that dash of pink and tangerine, the prism of sheer light on the gray-brown earth where the underpainting shines through an impossible chip in the world's enamel.

In Heat-Moon's Kansas, there are no such cracks or breaks. He walks the land's surface, learns its contours, understands in all its nuance and necessity that Chase County is cattle country. But Heat-Moon also perceives what lies beneath. Indeed, it's geology deeply buried that Heat-Moon sees as the beating heart of the beef industry above: "The chemical nature of the old seawater produced a stony land that produces good grasses that produce good, hoofed protein," he writes. "Flint Hills beef is a 250-million-year-old gift."

Kansans take deep pride in their cattle. But Heat-Moon finds reason for lament. "The linkings go no further back," he writes, "and the residents don't picture themselves as children of the Permian seas. They understand their living in the hills but not the hills living in them, and so the deeper links are broken." Heat-Moon encounters a socio-spiritual schism, a troubling disconnect between citizens and the land they love.

That schism may implicate each stone of the land, but it is not about geology alone. It is human. For Heat-Moon finds this, too: It is not only typical for Kansans to overlook the place's geologic past of ancient seas lapping at ancient shores, but also to cut history much shorter even than that, truncating the past at 1850.

"The sense of the past here is abbreviated," Heat-Moon writes, "and it lies separate like a severed limb." Heat-Moon finds in today's Chase County not only a refusal to remember the complexities of local Indigenous ways of being but a refusal to perceive in the Flint Hills any nonwhite history, present, or future.

This is where the kinship I found between Kansas and Douglas Island grows knotted. Or perhaps this is where it becomes clear, an emptiness weighing itself out. I think back to that cold spring in the Midwest when I recognized in the slow slant of the land the same rising elevation as my own island. But I am beginning to think that slant may be a cipher, the thought behind the thought.

▪ ▪ ▪

TRAVERSES (PART TWO): DOUGLAS ISLAND, USA

When I lived in Missouri, I heard a story on national radio about my hometown in Alaska. I learned this: In 1962 the City and Borough of Juneau devised a pretense by which to empty the Native village on Douglas Island, and then burned that village down. They cleaned up the site and built Douglas Harbor and the baseball diamonds that make up Savikko Park at the edge of Sandy Beach.

The story was new to me.

Yet during summers as a teen and then twenty-something, I launched and landed multi-week kayak trips from the Douglas Harbor over, and over, and over. Before that, springtimes, I played little league in Savikko Park. And even before that, I went to preschool in Douglas. When the Taku Winds blew, my dad would pick me up early. He'd zip me into one of the neon snowsuits so many children wore in the eighties, put my little-kid ski goggles onto my little-kid face, and take me down to Sandy Beach so that we could play in the winter storm. How the sand would fly! How the waves would crash! How our voices failed to thread the wind—how our thrill was reduced to pantomime! I remember crouching in clouds of flying sand, enthralled by pieces of beach ice, watching the wind and grit sculpt the ice grain by grain, Swiss-cheese divots deepening, widening. That sand and wind and salty ice were as alive as everything else I had ever seen in the world.

I realize now that I must have had classmates whose parents lost their own childhood homes in that city-sanctified fire. One lit right here in the place where the land taught me to perceive and answer to its inexplicable abundance.

But I did not know about the fire until I heard it on national radio as a solid piece of long-form reporting piped in to my middle Missouri living room from WBUR in Boston. I did not know the city had destroyed Native homes and disguised the deed by creating public spaces integral to my growing up, integral to my sense of place and ultimately belonging.

Now that I know, now what?

It occurs to me that we are in this together and that perhaps we are all, across ethnicities, warped by the omissions and the gaps left blank during our formative years. For myself, I am beginning to recognize silence as part of my most essential frame of reference. As part of that tear-shaped island in Alaska from which I take mark and measure of the world. Something that may have skewed my navigation ever since.

■ ■ ■

VECTOR NAVIGATION, A METHOD OF TRAVEL INVOLVING A PRECISE SEQUENCE OF COMPASS BEARINGS

In Chase County, Kansas, Indigenous history "lies separate like a severed limb"—so writes Heat-Moon. Do I see in the burning of the Douglas village one of my own community's histories lying separate like a severed limb as well? Yes. It's a history that needs public reckoning: a limb that some are working to reattach to the body of our story.

I, like many, grow disoriented among my own inheritances.

But in truth, my inheritances have been with me all along. New knowledge of the past doesn't actually change the present, just as new knowledge of a place does not change the terrain itself. It just changes our view of it. And the intimacy we bring to it.

I think of the men at the garage, the ones who took me in with my shivering dog, the men who wanted to hear about the hoot owl and the tumbleweeds and who, in turn, spoke of roots, live and strong, good beneath the morning frost. Those men love the land. As I do.

But what I learn from Heat-Moon is that the land is fundamentally geologic. Scientifically, spiritually, and metaphysically. In my eyes, Heat-Moon's difficult stance is this: to love a place based solely on one's experience of it—even based solely on a whole generation's experience of it—this love may be small-minded.

Not necessarily wrong, but small.

Because the land? It goes deeper than all that. Deeper than me. Deeper than you. Deeper than your generation, and deeper than mine.

We could reorient. Individually. Collectively. From whatever historic sense we have now toward one that plunges farther, wider. Perhaps that is where reconciliations lie.

I think of the trick sailors use to decipher shapes in the far distance. Instead of straining to look at the thing itself, they shift the gaze off to the side and yield to the intelligence of the eye's peripheral vision. And so midwinter in Canada's Yukon, reading about Chase County in the Flint Hills of Kansas, thinking about Douglas Island in the archipelago of Southeast Alaska, my mind shifts to the side. I revisit the kinship I felt one day while crossing open prairie. Of course I run through the facts: On a cold mid-continent spring day I recognized in the slow slant of the land the tilt of my own island. But I think that slow slant is only the thought behind the thought. To recognize my community in a distant one—to recognize correspondence between a foreign place and my own home—what does this recognition make possible?

■ ■ ■

SEVERANCES

I have coastal roots where the sea twice daily rakes the shores with twenty feet of tidal rising and falling. I am primed to scan the beach for marks of high and low tide. When the painter and I circle the gallery together, I scan the beaches she's put onto canvas. Curious about the painting's golden band of rocky shore, I ask about it. The golden band down there, by the water. That narrow, too-bright patch of yellow marking a far-off part of the beach. What is the golden dash on the far rocks?

The painter says it is a lichen. It is a near-neon lichen that grows on parts of Svalbard's beaches where commercial whalers used to bring their harvest and render whale fat. Like any lichen, this one lives on rock and air—but unlike most other lichens, this one also lives on the trace nutrients left by rendering whale blubber. So it is that on the beaches of Svalbard, the painter learned to read history in the colorful growth on the rocks. She began to see in a lichen's near-neon luminosity life's constant reuse and recycling; its relentless rebirth.

Indeed, those harpooned whales? They are past, but they are also present, living on in lichen. Lichen that wouldn't grow without the spillage of rendered whale fat. Fat that wouldn't spill without the hunting skill of the whalers. Whalers who wouldn't hunt without an economy's demand. So it is that a near-neon yellow lichen marks the Svalbard beach's deeper links (as Heat-Moon would say), reminding us that how it is now is always a close cousin to how it was then.

The painter and I muse: History inhabits all corners of the present. And we suppose that if those harpooned whales live on in the lichen, then in a sense the commercial whaling industry lives on in it, too.

■ ■ ■

ARRIVALS

Heat-Moon's essay on the ancient Nemaha Mountains underlying Kansas—it doesn't end with the severed limb of Indigenous history. It ends with a suturing. It ends with a stone.

In the essay, Heat-Moon searches the ground for a telltale chip of Precambrian granite from the ancient Nemaha Ridge. He seeks a talisman of the place's deep, ancient history. But he finds none.

Instead, Heat-Moon recognizes a piece of cryptocrystalline quartz. Cryptocrystalline quartz, colloquially called flint, is the rock for which the Flint Hills of eastern Kansas are named. He picks it up. Ponders it. Pockets it.

Geologists don't really know why spongy, sedimentary limestone laid down at the bottom of tropical seas lends itself to forming hard nodules of flint, but it does. Embedded in these mountaintop layers of Kansas are flakes of rock-hard certainty that, when struck, let fly the seeds of fire. Flint, reflects Heat-Moon, is "fire from the old sea."

Now with a shard of flint in his palm (a shard "the color of deep seawater under clouds"), Heat-Moon turns again toward the severance he's observed, the division between contemporary residents' truncated consciousness of the Flint Hills and the deep history of the Flint Hills. "Before the children of Europe took these hills," he writes, "the people who walked here believed stones to be alive because they carried heat, changed their forms, and moved if you watched them long enough. To them, rocks were concentrations of power and life." I ache all the more acutely when I read this. Rocks *were* concentrations of power and life. Sentiments that ring true, but that are cast into a grammatic past tense, give me the eerie feeling the world has already disappeared.

By pondering a piece of flint, the essay reattaches the severed limb of Chase County's history. Indeed, deep generations knew this land far before it became cattle country. They knew its sandy face, its rocky depths. They knew its shards of flint. Heat-Moon picks up one such sea-colored shard, recognizes the old knowledge of its heat, and with that, opens a line of sight onto history flowing freely again, rolling along 1850 as part of a much longer shoreline, an edge like any other, with certain points of inflection redirecting everything to come—but not an endpoint itself.

And therefore, not a beginning either. As neither conclusion nor origin, 1850 rejoins a larger continuity, a point in time both as elastic and as vital as many others.

■ ■ ■

RELOCATION

Refracting beams of light come from different starting points, different frameworks, different lines of sight. Via geometry and optics, they refract all the clear air of what-is with their varying angles, their incrementally varied tonal shifts.

Aloud, in the spacious art gallery, I wonder what points of reference direct the painting's refracting beams of light to the shore.

The painter has some ideas. People who called Svalbard home would have come to these shores to hunt, seeking cyclic sustenance. People who called themselves explorers would have come on accident, seeking to understand the bounds of the world and even the universe. People whose livelihood depended on industries of trade and commerce would have left their families to come for profit. Political needs would have driven some; others would have answered to desire and demand for substance anywhere on the spectrum from material to spiritual, existential.

Frameworks coincide. Edges cut against corners. Stories intersect, inflect one another's tellings. Through time and over distance, reference points meet on the shore in the strangest pink-orange, a flash, a prism of coincidence.

But ultimately, we can only guess. We can only guess at the points of reference clapping in invisible convergence upon the shore where the painter staked her strings, melted her wax, built temporary navigational prisms, all the while asking, *Where am I? Where did others come from to arrive just so, right here?*

▪ ▪ ▪

INFRASOUND

Come close to the painting. Draw near, as I inevitably did. With proximity, willful or otherwise, the world changes.

There is still a bare brown beach in the foreground. Bare—but for a narrow gold band crossing a far section of the rocky shore's clean browns. And at the edge of the mostly bare, brown beach still lies blue-gray water.

Up close, I still recognize that water's gray glass as the color of my old ache. I still recognize its surface. A surface lying upon depths.

Across the water in the painting's far plane, mountain slopes of blue-gray snow and brown-gray cliff still rise into the sky. I wonder who knows those ridgelines, who has felt that exact far shore's scree slopes shifting underfoot. I wonder how they found a way up, how they found a way down. And above those mountains still stretches a blue-gray sky filled with milk-gray clouds, bellies shadowed to pale slate.

And still, as frozen in their transience as the landmasses they traverse, three beams of refracted light. Crossing all planes of the canvas, converging in a pink prism upon the near plane of brown beach.

Viewed from a comfortable near distance, the painting remains a semi-abstracted landscape—a portrait of a clear, spare place crossed by a geometric, or optical, idea. But stand nose to nose with it. Now, see hairlines of bright color pop from the edge of every single shape on the canvas. Pink rims all the rocks of the shore, along with cadmium and scarlet. Red and lemon dashes hold depth in the clouds. Bolts of tangerine skim the far shore.

Remember that a typical underpainting is invisible. Remember that it is the first layer of color to meet the canvas; that it then governs the tone of all the colors laid down atop it. It is like the painter's private method of navigating the color wheel. But in this particular image, the underpainting shows through in hairline fissures exceeding every edge. Up close every rock and every whisp of cloud brims with refracted light, the spectrum split open.

Of proximity, essayist Ander Monson writes: "Get close enough to a thing and it becomes impossible to keep the whole in sight, to retain whatever belief you had before." The landscape painting cut by optical beams becomes, up close, a theory of light brimming over—of light, which is life—brimming over in rocks, in clouds, in the snowpack. Up close, Whitmanesque multitudes course through this spare, clear place while past, present, and future collide every day with cold air. The light, irreparably, is bent. It breaks. Color flashes.

The artist explains how her method creates visual depth. She directs me to stand back and adopt a normal distance; I see none of the bright colors of the underpainting, no cadmium bolts, no tangerine fissures. But now I do see how each rock on the beach seems to rise from the canvas into the still air of the gallery.

The land is like that, you know—always telling you things. It's like the past: persistent. But it's also like a reckoning, elusive.

Think of yourself as a child. An aching child who yearns for the spare, clear places. And permit yourself, however small you were all that time ago, to float in a kayak on protected, glacial lake waters. Reach for what drifts alongside. Tap a feather, a chip of ice, anything small and afloat and totally temporary, just like you. Tap it to see how, exactly, it rides the lake's surface, the one answering to the other as only a mirror can to the knotted sky.

SISTER ESSAYS: THE YOUNG AND THE OLD

I. The Young

PINPOINT DIFFUSED

Of all the geologic maps, my favorites are the terrane maps. Along the northwestern edge of North America, terrane maps depict warped bands and blocks of accumulated bedrocks, crustal material accreted onto other crusts. Terrane maps of North America's "Accretionary Belt" reveal our most essential foundation to be a jumble, a loosely tangled smear, a twist of fragments grafted onto moveable edges.

This geologic reality underpins a vast region. It is the story of the Saint Elias Range shared along the borderlands of eastern Alaska and western Yukon, of the whole southwestern half of Yukon, of all Southeast Alaska, and virtually all of British Columbia.

My focus lies at the heart of this area. Center lies here, in the tripart borderlands of northern Southeast Alaska, southern Yukon, and northern British Columbia.

It is the place to which I belong by birth. It is the place to which I belong by lifestyle, by permanent address. But I am considering a new idea of origins today—that is, that I come not from place alone. That I come also from a family lineage and that mine is a lineage of people displaced. That I come, then, from a human current, and a restless one which, for all its own tumult of displacement, displaced and displaces others.

I am considering this very seriously—though I feel, every day, that I am at home.

And so I try to understand this dissonance of belongings by enlarging my sense of things overall. Indeed, what happens when one so enlarges one's notion of "the center," taking a geographic and temporal enormity—with ambiguous edges at that—as "central"?

THE THING BROKE APART

At its surface the planet is crust, two kinds: continental and oceanic. Fifteen or so main plates in all. One can make a portrait of the planet by sketching its jagged net of fault lines, charting the world as a restless complex of spaces between.

But in ancient times, before anyone could decipher the earth in terms of its own liminal edges, the plates we would recognize as continents today were clasped together as a single landmass: Pangea, which translates to "all earth" in Greek. And all that land was surrounded by a single unbounded ocean: Panthalassa, "all sea."

The earth has changed since then. For as the core principle of plate tectonics holds, the earth's crust never sleeps in its search of the world's edge. And so this arrangement of one Ur-continent surrounded by one Ur-ocean was a temporary unity. The thing broke apart. Its pieces remain in motion, restless. So it is that these plates of the earth's crust creep and roar. So it is that these plates of the earth's crust rove atop the earth's mantle, that subterranean and molten deep about which Dante in his *Inferno* may have already recorded everything we can know with any certainty.

NOW

Now Pangea is broken. Now Panthalassa is split. Now the earth is made of two Americas, of Europe and Asia, of Africa, Australia, Antarctica, and of oceans between them.

But of course this is temporary, a frozen image, a still life.

The thing broke apart. It's been in motion ever since.

Shot, reverse shot, and action: The Americas draw away from Europe and Africa. Magma rises from a rift in the sea floor, the Mid-Atlantic Ridge. Cooling magma creates new oceanic crust. The planet's expansion in the Atlantic plays the yang to the yin of contraction in the Pacific. There, the Pacific Plate jams into the western edge of the Americas and subducts, dense basaltic seafloor inching underground into the molten deep underlying all the earth's crust as we know it. Grinding its way down under the continental edge of North America, the Pacific Plate feeds itself into the mantle like a sheet of steel into a furnace.

My part of the world lies here, at the western edge of North America, where the subducting Pacific Plate not only moves mountains but makes them. Here, the Pacific Plate curves and crumbles in an ongoing plunge, thrusting all that lies above farther and farther skyward. Here, mountains rise as continually transformed as steam. Here, we cannot forget that inherent in transformation is loss.

A MAP IS A PORTRAIT

I am invested in tracing origins. And in charting foundations. That means I am invested in the question of how my part of the world got to be the way it is now (process). And it means that I search for its constants, its steadiest components, those making up its throughlines and continuities (material).

Terrane cartographers depict my part of the world with colors and two-letter abbreviations like childhood initials. The Yukon-

Tanana Terrane (YT) makes a slender green *V* like a downward-slanted two-tined fork. Wedged in deep between the tines of YT is the olive-tinted Stikine Terrane (ST). And the purple-hued ribbons of the Alexander Terrane (AX) and Wrangellia (WR) drape in a loose tangle along the length of the southwestern tine.

Only in much larger scale maps, far zoomed in to the northern part of AX, do terrane cartographers specify smaller bedrocks, like the Gravina Belt. On these, Gravina appears as a brown dash among surrounding purples. It is situated just a couple purple shades southwest of the green-and-olive bands above. The Gravina Belt includes, at roughly its center, the rainforested island on which I was raised.

I peer at terrane maps, wondering how the world got to be the way it is. Wondering what, if anything, has ever held steady.

Gravina is an area of volcanic crustal material that was formed here, in place. Accreted limestones surround it on all sides. In other words, Gravina is a strangely local bedrock. Strange, because fragments with distant origins sandwich it. In fact, it is due to the geologic mayhem of crashing and smearing limestone accretion that Southeast Alaska became a site of profound crustal disturbance in the first place, disturbance which opened the rift through which magma flowed straight up to form the volcanic "intrusion" that formed the Gravina Belt.

For Gravina, collision opened the possibility of inception itself. Gravina only exists, really, because of other conflicts. Because of a crashing, one so terrible it tore open the earth.

But in geologic understandings of the world, crashing is not so uncommon. It is a basic mechanism of creation.

METAPHOR

I must be forthright. Bedrock geology grips my mind because I believe in metaphor. The notion that beneath our feet lies an adamantly scientific, adamantly poetic enormity, a solidified one that makes up the literal foundation of every single thing anyone has ever built—from buildings to beliefs—it's attractive.

THE ESSENTIALS OF STONE AND SLOPE

Here is a story from ancient Greece. The gods condemn King Sisyphus (cunning traitor and thief) to a backbreaking task, eternal by design: He must push a boulder up a mountain. But the boulder is under a spell cast by Zeus, and so it slips from Sisyphus's grasp just shy of the summit, teeters, and goes crashing back down the slope. Sisyphus must descend and begin the task anew. The punishment is partly in the pain of physical toiling, but especially in the fate of endless repetition.

Understood in terms of the human condition, the story wrestles with themes of useless labor and the continual shouldering and re-shouldering of impossible burdens.

But the boulder interests me more than Sisyphus. Let us home in, then, on the story's lesser-recognized essentials: the essentials of stone and slope. The essentials of perpetual movement, of ceaseless physical forces in and upon the land.

THEY LIVE AND DIE AND LIVE AND DIE

The North American continent—and significantly, the continental edge on which the Alaska/Yukon/British Columbia borderlands developed—used to be elsewhere. On the planet. Specifically, this region of the North American continent used to be tropical.

Wrap your mind around it if you can. I cannot.

But to see these subarctic mountains for what they are, you must accept this: The whole place used to be someplace else. Geologically, the place is a kind of newcomer in its own present.

Paradox, or cyclic nature of oppositions?

Tracing this subarctic lineage takes us south.

Tracing this mountainous lineage takes us underwater.

So be it. Throw your mind to the tropics. Find a warm, shallow sea lapping an equatorial continent's shore—North America to be, for example, or regions of Eurasia. In either case the sea is rich with light, with algae. It is rich with corals and mollusks, too—that is, it is filled with crinoidal life, with echinoderms. Make in your mind a bright aqueous place busy with everyone who builds their homes and bones of calcium.

This everyone, the everyone who builds their homes and bones of calcium, they live and die and live and die. Generations pass. Species evolve. Every day, broken sea bones and vacant sea houses sift down through shafts of light. Settle on the seafloor. Fine beach mud builds up in million-year graveyards.

Over time, layer upon layer of calcium fragments and grains solidify. Become limestone. Become rock. Under a warm, shallow sea dancing with rays of light, fine carbonate beach mud solidifies to stone.

LOCATION

Calcified in me are at least two kinds of histories, both mine and not-mine. There is "my history," as in my family history. Genetics, stories. And there is "my history," as in the history of Southeast Alaska and its neighbors. Politics, cultures, ecologies.

Is it a question of the body? Perhaps my body stands "in" a history the same way it stands "in" a place.

Essayist W. Scott Olsen also asks, "Where am I?" Upon reflection, Olsen posits that "perhaps this one question in the myriad forms it takes during the course of a life, during the course of a civilization, is why we are so in love with maps, why we pause in front of them, linger over them without a prior question. A map is a promise, a pledge to pin something down just long enough to see it."

But a terrane map is the kind of map we look to not simply to ask "Where am I?" but also "When?" and even "How?" This is to say, a terrane map is a portrait of deep history in present place. In this sense a terrane map is certainly a *promise*. But it is less a pledge to *pin* down so much as it is a pledge to *dive* down or *reach* deep—suggesting a perception of place rooted in ancientness. Suggesting an ancientness integrated into a present quite literally built from and upon it.

ARCHIVES

The specific histories of these warm, well-lit seas, their turbidities and temperatures, their changes in depth and the lifeforms that thrived in them—all these stories are written into the stone, layer upon layer. This is to say that limestones the world over carry their genealogies, bear the traces, page by page, of their own histories.

I suppose I bear the same. Take a cross section of me. Closest to the sky, my loamy organics face the sun and wind with social cyclicality, integrated and inseparable from roots and mycelia and detritivores and the footsteps of all those who scuffle my surface. Deeper down are my layers of sand and stone, layers through which water percolates, layers otherwise secret. Deeper still, the impermeable clays on which these were all laid down. The layers through which nothing may pass, but on which the active layers depend.

Somewhere around these depths of my cross section is the generation that fled European antisemitism. Look at it closely to see the generations that migrated, learned to work American soil. See the precise generation that changed its religion, its language, its name. See the generations that played their insignificant, essential roles in the land grab of America's westward expansion. To see this is to see how my ancestors' flight from European oppressions bound them to American ones. Bound *me* to American ones. Such origins do feel geologic at the end of the day, impermeable if not impenetrable. Buried, in any case—far from individuality, from lived life. Yet integral.

As for individuality, my origins are these: I was born in an early winter storm at the foot of a great mountain. It was one mountain among many, many others. I was one baby among four or five others the same night. I guess it wasn't a good birth, and for that I am sorry. My mother touched death, but it's okay because she lived—the wind and sleet and crashing sea must have smiled. For who can resist smiling for a baby? And so off I sailed into infancy with one mother and one father and one cat and three dogs upon the endless earth.

I wonder if infant-me ever would have believed you if you'd said the world was moving underfoot, that it always has been. That the best any of us ever get on this caroming planet is the fleeting approach of balance, a teetering atop what exceeds us.

PLATE TECTONICS

Massive limestone deposits formed offshore of these parts of North America when it was tropical, around 350 million years ago. But the whole of North America shifted. It went north. Gradually, the seas lapping its shores were no longer tropical, but temperate. And subarctic. And even Arctic. North went the continent, offshore limestone formations in tow. These limestones would later uplift to form the entire southwest half of now-Canada's Yukon Territory (as well as now-British Columbia's inland).

Older limestone deposits also formed off shorelines far from ancient North America. Some, deposited some 450 million years ago on the other side of the planet, were dragged inch by inch across the globe until they coincided—and collided—with North America. These limestones would uplift to form virtually all of now-the-US's Southeast Alaska.

PULLING ROCK FROM SEA TO SKY

That is how massive crustal fragments of tropical limestones came from Eurasia to North America, "exotic" limestones smashing into "local" ones. Accretion, this.

For the dense basaltic seafloor remains much heavier than the limestone terranes deposited in layers upon it. And so as the Pacific Plate subducts under North America, various of its transported limestones float, smearing as a scud of foam along the continent while the leading edge of the Pacific Plate grinds down into the mantle, rejoining the earth's molten places.

Subduction is tumultuous. The crashing, the buckling, the torquing and heaving and toppling—it raised mountains.

Subduction of the Pacific Plate raised North America's Coastal Range. Subduction of the smaller but related Yakutat microplate raised the northernmost of these, the Saint Elias Mountains: On the Southeast Alaska/British Columbia border, Mount Fairweather rises over 15,000 feet above sea level. Next door in Yukon, Mount Logan reaches a bit more than 19,500 feet.

I wonder at this, at the force capable of pulling rock from the sea into the sky.

In any case, all in all, this vertical, forested, ice-capped land is not so old. For one, its constituent limestones were formed only a few hundred million years ago. They come from the Paleozoic Era, from its Ordovician to its Carboniferous periods. And their uplifting from the seafloor into skyward mountains is even more recent. Geologists assure us the most certain and solid features of this part of the world, the mountains, were made during only the last fifteen million years or so. They are phenomena of the geologic present, the Cenozoic.

INTRUSIONS

It is interesting that both geologists and preachers will tell you there's only so far a person can descend before reaching the pure fire that boils underfoot.

But while the preachers emphasize fire, geologists emphasize the boiling. Because that subducting Pacific Plate—it's the bottom of the sea. It's wet. As wet, bottom-of-the-sea rock scrapes down under the lip of the continent, down into a more molten part of our planet, sea-moisture joins with magma. Geologists assure us that water changes everything down there. Rock boils differently, expands differently, explodes differently. And so it is that many volcanoes, pressurized vents through which great surges of molten rock rise and spread upon the land, intrude upon this accretionary region with their own signature bedrocks.

I was raised on one such volcanic intrusion.

The Gravina Belt.

This could become, I fear, a geologic metaphor for newcomers onto this land; a metaphor of arrivals and displacements. I think of settler-colonial arrivals, settler-colonial displacements of Indigenous peoples.

The first in-migrating generation lands and stays: an uneasy echo of accretion.

Then the second generation, born in place, emerges as if from the earth itself: it hatches underfoot, like volcanic material originating right there—yet originating there because of colliding forces, thus strangely bound both to the place and to not-the-place.

I am disappointed when rock is reduced to metaphor. Still, when I, a second-generation Alaskan, learn that my beautiful childhood unfolded largely on an "intrusive" formation, I am crestfallen. I think, *There is power in language*.

STUBBORNNESS

Gravina Belt, intrusive volcanic formation of my home island—please do not stand up as a metaphor for the facts of my existence. Take me as metaphor instead. I have a mind full of stubbornness and a too-sharp heart and a skeleton made of bones. Surely something in me is hard enough, foundational enough, to repurpose into an insight about this island's long, spiny shore, the rock of its chill, lichened ridgelines, the great gray blocks pulled from the quarries of its belly.

ORIGINS

How did this come to be? The earth; the world?

Essayist Esmé Weijun Wang offers a three-part inventory. "Pan Gu the giant slept in an egg-shaped cloud; once released he formed the world with his blood, bones, and flesh," she writes. "God said, 'let there be light.' Ymir was fed by a cow who came from ice." Those are some ways, among many others, that the world came to be.

What of this part of the earth, this northwest area of North America?

Origins-oriented poets and ethnographers, for example, call my part of the world the Raven Biome. It's the Raven's caprice that brings the world to be.

Geologists call it the Accretionary Belt; a world made of rocks in turn rafting, smearing, subducting, and uplifting.

We all need a starting place. That is why everyone carries explanations of beginnings, holding them close. Because, as Wang writes, "*How did this come to be?* is another way of asking, *why did this happen?*, which is another way of asking, *what do I do now? But what on earth do I do now?*"

HAUNTINGS

The myth of Sisyphus: a tale of endless suffering, or a tale of the living, driven, cyclic, animate earth? Geologists, what say you?

Classically understood, the human occupies center stage while the rock and the slope are metaphors built to expand the story's human significance. In this reading, the tale speaks to the psyche's inescapable burdens. It speaks to the futility that haunts human life. But I propose a reversal of roles, a reading in which the rock and the slope hold central significance and the human operates as a metaphor crafted in service of expanding earthly significance.

If we displace the futility and eternity of human struggle from the story's center, if we call those human elements scaffolding and turn instead to the boulder and to the slope of the mountainside, I believe the Greeks have given us a touchstone of spiritual ecology and earth science all in one. For this tale of a stone in perpetual motion, a stone enchanted by Zeus, a stone inhabited—if you will—by the divine: Does it not anticipate erosion, deposition, even the enormous incremental vitality of plate tectonics? Does it not speak one clear line straight to the earth's crust itself as an eternally animate being? Does it not suggest we walk every day upon the living?

Geologists, I have watched you sideways from a crack in my eyelid no bigger than a mote of dust. I have seen what you do when the rest of us are sleeping; I have seen you bend beyond all known edges to glimpse the life inherent in rock.

GENEALOGY OF STONE

Who is it that says so beautifully: For diasporic people, the journey, the movement, *is* home? In any case it occurs to me that we diasporic people, like everyone else, have reason to see the earth as our closest kin.

THE YOUNG AND THE OLD

Around here, we remind each other this is young land. We mean it. Like all places, this place came from someplace else.

We also say this place is unimaginably old. Indeed, Indigenous peoples have been here since time immemorial. The place I was born and raised belongs to the Áak'w K̲wáan Tlingit. T'aak̲u K̲wáan lands are adjacent, just south toward the Taku River. In the other direction, up Lynn Canal lies Jilk̲aat Tlingit country. And across the Coastal Range lie Southern Tutchone territories, the lands of Tagish peoples, and of various inland Tlingit groups. People have always been at home here. Since the beginning. Forever.

Indeed, on the inland side of these vast Coast Mountains, they say prehistoric peoples lived with neighbors like short-faced bears and woolly mammoths and giant beavers alongside a vast sheet of ice. That before the land was forested it was a subarctic savannah, the brief summers' bunchgrasses rustling with all kinds of people's jokes and prayers, obligations and stories, their questions, their disappointments. That on the coastal side of the mountains maritime cultures grew and sang, pounded drums so powerful even the ice sheet listened. That all across these borderlands, winter has always made a good home here, and that since the beginning of time the snowpack has creaked under the weight of people who pause, as all people do, to consider the night sky.

Young land that is unimaginably old—yes. The place is geologically new. The place is humanly ancient. After all, as the basic principle of stereoscopic vision holds, it is only by combining two simultaneous lines of sight, each anchored to its distinct and separate point of origin, that we can see with depth.

Look! There goes planet earth, for billions of years, perpetually becoming as it now is; perpetually becoming what it will be next.

Watch: Here it comes round again.

Then came the present, and now it is the future.

II. The Old

There were so many caribou it looked like the mountain was moving.
—Yukon Ice Patch Project, consulting Elder

Ancient hunters hike into the alpine to get the caribou congregating there. Hunters have darts until they have bows and arrows. They have bows and arrows until they have muskets that don't work well so they keep using bows and arrows. Then they have rifles and these replace bows and arrows the way that bows and arrows replaced darts.

There are two things to notice across millennia like these. First, things keep changing. Second, the people and the caribou go way back. They go way, way back. They always have.

But by the time of rifles, the caribou seem to be fewer, or elsewhere, or gone. Stories of herds so thick they looked not like herds but like the earth itself, not like animals moving upon the mountain but like the mountain itself rousing into action—as I understand it, those are stories the Elders recount from their own Elders. No one living saw caribou in numbers like that.

For myself, they are stories I read about in a book. "There were so many caribou it looked like the mountain was moving," I read, glossy page resting on my two fingertips.

But that is all in the future. For now, the mountain moves with caribou upon the land. The mountain moves from land within the caribou. As I understand it, darts then arrows then bullets fly like needles and thread, attaching, reattaching, binding, joining human to caribou, caribou to human.

▪ ▪ ▪

For a year, I live across the border from Alaska among my Yukon neighbors—people, mountains, caribou. And ancestors too, I should think. Which raises a question I could have asked in Alaska, or everywhere I've ever been, but did not think of until now. What, specifically, is my relationship to the past people of the place I'm in? To the people who knew caribou in such numbers that it looked like the mountain was moving?

▪ ▪ ▪

For months of deep winter the northern land sleeps. It's frozen and still. But under the snowpack the land is quietly fat, swollen.

Springtime thaws come.

Mosquitoes hatch in clouds. So do black flies, horse flies, white socks, no-see-ums. The land splits open in a hot rush. So it was then, so it is now. Cycles abound and patterns course through time like rivers. People know the mosquitoes will hatch. Caribou know too.

People rub aspen dust on their faces from the bark of pale pea-colored trees. They burn smoky fires. They adjust. So do the caribou, who retreat upvalley. They move into the cooler, breezier alpine. They find windswept ridgelines. They find fields of summer ice.

Ice patches.

And they gather there in massive herds, raft the main current of the wind, push their soft noses into the snow.

Later begin the night frosts, frosts harder night by night, each night intercepted by the soaking warmth of autumn's afternoon sun. Thus come mountainsides gone scarlet with the turning leaves of dwarf birch. Thus come river valleys traced in gold with turning aspen leaves.

It's always like this: a green, thrumming summer, air thick with urgent insects, caribou herds finding refuge in alpine winds and on ice patches. That all leads right into the red and golden fall. Then the red and golden fall closes right down to winter, fully silver. Silver and cold rose. Home.

■ ■ ■

Those fields of alpine ice where caribou convene in the summer to cool off? They begin, of course, with snow. It accumulates all winter in high cirques and alpine bowls. Springtime, ever cavalier, disrupts the land's sleep and makes the winter snowpack groan and creak and go, bit by bit, to mush. Snow melts, feeding watersheds all summer long.

That is how winter takes care of us year-round.

But not all the winter snow melts. Some places it accumulates year after year. It grows. It grows heavy. The snow's crystalline structure buckles under its own weight, crushed into ice so dense it's blue. This is first how ice is made and second how ice becomes glacial.

When ice accumulates and grows deep and wide like a lake, we call it an icefield. And when an icefield spills over one mountainous edge or another, sending a sinuous tongue of ice to answer the siren call of gravity, we call that flowing river of ice a glacier. Night after night, licking the ears of the mountains, glaciers grind and crush and sculpt and transport and pulverize and scrape. These are the verbs we use to explain Southeast Alaska's fjord country, for example. Those actions explain the shape of the steep land and cold sea I come from.

But among our inland neighbors in Yukon, I learn that glacial grinding, pulverizing, and surging is only one stance among others. There are quieter ways for ancient ice to hold itself. Sometimes snow compresses to ice in high alpine bowls—but accumulates with less volume than we tend to see coastally. Sometimes this forms not a lake of ice filling a mountain range and spilling in great currents off its precipitous ledges—but simply a pond. Glaciologists call these "ice patches."

Where an icefield is like a lake and a glacier is like a river pouring out, an ice patch is more like a teacup. It is a teacup of ancient ice, resting on its high alpine saucer.

Yukon is home to many ice patches. So is Norway. So is Sweden, and so are the Alps. Even Montana, Colorado, and Wyoming have their share of ice patches. And so does Alaska. Because ice patches are relatively small—less susceptible to flowing with gravity, surging and waterfalling across the land—they inspire robust archaeological studies the world over.

Think of it this way: Where a glacier pulverizes and wrenches and crushes and torques, an ice patch simply sits. Maybe it hums a solitary note. And sustains it. Forever.

Quietude is the key to ice patch archaeology. What's frozen into an ice patch is held safe. What's frozen into an ice patch has been neither ground nor crushed nor dragged in the belly of a glacier across miles of bone-breaking terrain. In an ice patch, anything frozen in has been encased. It has been immobilized, suspended, placed on pause, enshrined. What's embedded in an ice patch is simply held, ice and object nested somewhere on the continuum of eternity like folded hands, the one resting in the other.

■ ■ ■

First there were darts then there were bows and arrows then there were muskets then there were rifles. In southern Yukon, all this movement—all this living and dying—circled round and round against the backdrop of those ice patches' soundless hum. And on the ice patches summered the caribou, pushing their soft noses in the snow.

Ancient people didn't live up by the ice patches. They camped down in the valleys. But hunters hiked steep slopes to harvest caribou in the alpine where they gathered by the thousands, pushing their soft noses around in the snow. Plus, the ice patches made for good refrigeration. After a successful hunt, the hunters could store meat on the ice. They could bring down enough to feed the family for a time, then return to the ice patch for more later without losing the meat to rot.

When it was time, family groups would congregate in late summer at fish camps. They would work together through the fall to get fish. Then they would disperse again in winter, spreading themselves more thinly out over the land.

Archaeologists and anthropologists call this rhythm "semi-nomadic," stressing the impermanence of the peoples' settlements, and indicating migratory movement between seasonal villages and campsites. But I think that in describing "home" as a series of temporary sites, we miss the expansiveness right in front of our noses. Another way to look at it: People here lived in a home so big it took all year to inhabit the whole of it.

▪ ▪ ▪

Just north of Whitehorse's Two Mile Hill, you can turn off the Alaska Highway and drive uphill through the forest to Fish Lake, which lies in Category A Settlement Lands of the Kwanlin Dün First Nation. A short hike takes you up a sometimes-braided, sometimes-muddy trail that quickly leaves the treeline and opens into the alpine. There is a saddle, a ridge, two small peaks you can pop up to along the ridgeline, and then a steep drop-off. From the ridge, you can look down and out over Fish Lake in one direction or out over the Bonneville Lakes and toward the Boundary Mountains in the other.

I think about caribou so thick it looked like the whole mountain was moving because almost as soon as I arrived in Yukon, in the fall, out at Fish Lake, I saw one. Movement on the side of the mountain, movement with a luxurious white throat. Caribou. Browsing downslope. Tawny flank, turn of nose, flick of tail, and ripple of shoulder. Hooves crunching lichen and dwarf birch, knees ankles stifles flexing and bending, stepping through wind. The weight of antlers. And the easy path it traced along the slow slope of the mountain. Yes, that most of all: everything converging on ease.

I returned to Fish Lake many times during my Yukon year. Sometimes I saw no caribou. Other times I saw a moving row of specks, a small herd moving across the frozen Bonneville Lakes one valley over. I would watch the thread of caribou spider its way along the lake and think about how, not far from here, it used to be that the mountain itself seemed to move. People saw it. Their descendants tell the stories from when it was so.

I often find myself alone yet surrounded in this way. Alone on a mountain, alone but for the dog. Surrounded by everyone else; dwarf birch, lichen, wind, a caribou. Covering small distances in my pensive exuberant cautious way. Listening and watching for movement, for animals, for weather, for the shape of the land I might follow next time. Alone with a cresting sense the cold air I breathe only *looks* clear. Alone with the sense that in reality the cold air is thick with everyone who has ever been here, and that we are, quite seriously, here together.

I know now that people have been at Fish Lake for a long time. People have been sitting on these rocks, walking this land, looking at caribou, and harvesting them—for generations and generations and generations. And I have questions about life in this kind of contact zone, where we are all entangled with other forms of life. Are we not also entangled with the past? With past lives? Do we not . . . have truck with the ancients who lived on the land we walk? I need to know how courteous regard can reach not only across species but by necessity also across time.

■ ■ ■

In southern Yukon as in Alaska, as everywhere else on earth, ice that hasn't melted for thousands of years is, in these past and present decades, turning to water and draining downhill. Very, very rapidly—though not all at once. The edge softens first.

In the nineties, alpine ice melting in Yukon uncovered ground previously enshrined for millennia. And people started finding things. Old things; past lives.

The first alpine find on newly uncovered ground: a smell like a barnyard.

It came from a thick black loamy area at the base of an ice patch. And it was doubly significant for the Dall sheep hunters who found it. Not only was it the most massive deposit of caribou dung they had ever seen, but caribou had been absent from those mountains, the mountains west of Kusawa Lake, for decades.

And so they knew it was old. They knew biologists would want to see for themselves. As would the people whose stories told of those very caribou. The sheep hunters brought word of the high alpine barnyard scent, the field of scat rimming a melting ice patch.

Subsequent searching along the edge of the same ice patch yielded a short wooden stick with a piece of string attached. There were even remnants of a feather jammed in under the sinew lashing.

Some scientists worked at carbon dating. Others came and took ice cores.

Was the caribou dung just on the surface of the ice patch? They wondered. Or was it distributed throughout many layers, suggesting caribou inhabited this place over the long-term? And what of the stick? Who made it, who attached the piece of string—and when?

The caribou dung deposit came in between two and three thousand years old.

The stick and string, five thousand.

Boreal forest soils are acidic. Organic materials dropped there break down. Digging in the dirt, archaeologists find little else apart from stone blades, dart tips, and arrowheads. Digging in the dirt, there is no ancient caribou dung. There are no ancient strings, no ancient sticks. So it is that the edge of this ice patch altered archaeology in the Yukon.

The Yukon Ice Patch Project was born. Biologists and archaeologists partnered with the region's First Nations culture and heritage organizations, their venerated knowledge bearers, their youth. Teams began monitoring ice patches, surveying their perimeters, analyzing ice cores and artifacts, lining up all the new finds alongside all the old stories.

Ice patch archaeology yields bone. Antler. Wood. Dung. Sinew lashings. The intricacy of a feather. Living tissues. Pliable, sensate, eager.

■ ■ ■

In the time of darts, hunters shot caribou with throwing boards or atlatls. Like any tool, the atlatl transforms the body, transforms what it can do. Throwing boards and atlatls heightened accuracy, force, distance. Magnified mind and movement. Bridged the caribou's transformation from flesh to meat, from animal to food, to shelter, to medicine, to strong tools, well made.

Most darts were tipped with large stone points. But on a visit to Yukon's archaeology and paleontology collections, weaving in and out of the stacks with a Yukon government archaeologist as my guide—I get to see one of the earliest found dart tips. And it is not made of stone at all. This dart tip is made of caribou antler.

Thin grooves nick its edges into barbs. It is pale and slender and it trembles, or maybe that is just the light. Yes. Maybe trembling is what light cannot help but do when it lands on something the color of cream that, having spent nine thousand years encased in ice, is just now melting out into the air we breathe today.

The Yukon government archaeologist and I look at the dart for a long time. *Nine thousand years old*, I repeat, as if this will help me absorb a sense of time. *Yes*, he answers, and I sense his mind is further along than mine is on this mystery of time and its depths. The dart tip is so slender, so slight, razor's edge curved and toothed. Presumably it was made by a hunter. Certainly it was made by a master carver, a maker, a sculptor.

The dart bears a carved pattern. It's small, about an inch long, a pattern of offset *s* curves. They overlap, like a braid. Like string. Like a DNA helix. Like the way skiers make figure eights of one another's turns. Like the ridgeline of far mountains reflected on a mirror of flat water. In any case, one set of curves answers the other. Identical and offset. A geometric pair carved in spatial tension.

■ ■ ■

About a carved wooden bird, John Berger writes: "One is looking at a piece of wood that has become a bird. One is looking at a bird that is somehow more than a bird. One is looking at something that has been worked with a mysterious skill and a kind of love."

That is carving. Something worked with mysterious skill and a kind of love into more than what sparked it.

"Not a symbol of a bird," specifies Berger, but an effort to "translate a message received from a real bird."

The dart tip is nine thousand years old. Left behind on alpine ice, it was encased, preserved. Then one day the melting ice let it go. Its curved edge is nicked into fine and deadly barbs. Its smooth surface bears a carved helix.

If Berger is right that the carved bird is not a symbol at all, and that we ought to see it instead as a translated message received from a real bird—then I suppose the dart's etched helix is not a symbol either but, similarly, a message. I suppose the dart's etched helix translates a message received from a real helix, a pattern of curves like airy fibers twisted robustly into rope, or like mountaintops answering the glass of a lake, or like the spiraling codes we inherit, and inherit, and inherit.

▪ ▪ ▪

Why are things the way they are?

There used to be so many caribou it was like the whole mountain was moving.

The etched spiral on the ancient dart moves too, rippling along bone.

Seasons turn. Daughters reflect their grandmothers, and water reflects the sky, and willow strips weave and wrap over and over into baskets filled with berries and then emptied. Caribou calves race to nowhere and kick up their heels. Everyone in the herd lifts their face to the breeze, fills their lungs in the high tundra cirques. They push their noses around in the snow to cool off. It feels good.

But if they glimpse approaching intruders, caribou spring so lightly on their hooves it's like they're not touching the earth at all. Always already weightless, a caribou. A reflection, it would seem, of air itself.

SWAN SIGNS

The swans are named for musicians: trumpeters. But I'll tell you whose psychedelics they do not sound like, not one bit. Dizzy Gillespie's. I have been listening to these buglers all day from the thawing edges of Marsh Lake and trumpeter swans sound mellow above all else, more like French horns. Their voices rise in warm timbres and round tones and have even a French horn's finicky intonation and tendency to crack. Nothing strident here. No fanfare, no bombast.

On and on and on, the swans warble all day. Dozens in the early season as the snow begins to melt. Then hundreds. A French horn choir blankets the boreal forest as the swans roll north. I know this because during migration season I frequent Swan Haven, a semi-rustic interpretive center in the Southern Lakes region of Canada's Yukon Territory. It's out at the edge of Marsh Lake's McClintock Bay, a half hour or so from

Whitehorse. Tucked well off in the trees, but not too far from the road.

Because there is, in fact, a road. Crossing Yukon's mountainous boreal forest, 575 miles of the Alcan Highway, built in the 1940s across northwestern Canada by the US military, slice southern Yukon end to end. Some say it shrank the land. That things changed with the road, things that haven't changed back.

Some say grief is a way to connect with what's lost.

At Swan Haven, a sequence of informational signs marks a beach walk along the edge of the lake. Each sign includes a panel of large text affixed to a wooden frame. Slumping sandbags weight the base of each frame against the wind. "Go for a walk!" reads the first sign.

And so I do. I go sign to sign, drinking the swan sounds in, and in, and in. As if these migrators would tell me something of their coming and going, and so something of the world's sheer girth. Or if not of its girth, at least of the porosity of its borders. And if they'll reveal nothing of girth nor of porosity, perhaps the swans can tell me something of the future. What's to come, for example, in this too-quickly warming springtime. How to traverse the muck of this sudden season. How to receive its abrupt change. How to carry on without winter's hard-packed stability. How to bend with the loss inherent in transformative times.

Perhaps eighty-five swans are around at the moment. I listen to them voicing their swanness on the ice, in the mud, on the water. I listen to the roll and creak of their chorus. The gentle busy continuity of sound wraps me in something I wish to trust.

Swan counts reported by the Yukon government's Wildlife Viewing Program earlier in the week were in the two hundreds, though a resident who lives on the adjacent shore tells me the official count is a lowball. *Counted five hundred sixty-five on Tuesday from my deck*, he confides. His counts are higher because he trains his spyglasses on the lake every evening at dusk, well after the end of the normal government employee work day. And the highest numbers are at dusk because they include the late evening arrivals, he says, before early morning departures shrink the numbers again.

Still, even with only eighty-five swans warble-bugling through the afternoon, their voices roll over the water, over the beach. They lay a sonic cushion across land troubled with a too-early melt. It mellows the forest's sharp smell of needles and sap. It mutes last winter's cracking ice. And is it just me, or does their sound even limber up the light? Listening to the swans, I swear the still-bare poplar branches stand one hair less brittle against the glass of the sky.

Spring is both the land's mourning and its resilience in the face of winter's letting go. But as great waves of swans begin to roll through the season's stiff fingers, pairs and pairs and pairs of them leapfrogging marshes and lakes, skies and wetlands, maybe the sense of loss starts to ease up. They are so loud and large and clean-looking, after all. And they come from so far.

I learn from the next swan sign, for example, that their migration is about a three-month journey. And they will sometimes travel hundreds of miles in a day. The curvature of the earth itself could take shape in facts like these, but the swan signs are not really meant for reverie. They bring it all back down to earth: "Swans can fly at speeds up to 80 kilometres an hour," reads one sign. "If you walked that fast you would get to the end of this trail in less than a minute!"

Well, no one walks that fast. But it is true that this is land of long crossings. People used to walk some four hundred miles one way to trading sites, then walk the same distance home. For generations, millennia, since time immemorial—on this land, people took long walks. What's more, it's never been only about people. Caribou herds seasonally cover a lot of ground as well, and migratory birds arrive every year from thousands of miles south. The cycles of travel are sweeping, vast, communal. They always have been.

Then a road came through.

This is still a land of vast crossings, of course. Everyone feels it, every day—the breadth, the distance, the inter-reliances crossing them. At the same time there are those who feel the road shrank the land. Stymied some of its vital movement, even. Fractured mutualities.

Now that there's a road, people don't really take long walks. They take long drives. *We* take long drives.

But sedentary life in these forests is a recent development. There are Elders who remember long walks from childhood, from before the road came through in the forties or before it magnetized semi-nomadic communities onto its crumbly edges in the years that followed. Those Elders remember, and they tell us stories, because how else would we know about life on the land, life lived in motion across great distances?

Plenty among us grieve what the road ruined, what it altered and did not restore. Yet the road is part of many of us. Me, for example. The road is why I thrive, apprenticing myself to the trails I find, a river here, a ridgeline there, learning from various people I encounter along the way. With my little gray truck of books and gear I have ease of travel and I'm safe enough, studying the questions that trouble me.

Such as, what balm is the sound of a swan? To a person who, like all people, squints to see farther? To a forest that, like all forests, rockets into a strange new climate? What balm *is* the sound of a swan?

I heard recently of a certain fox, one who did not have to squint to see, who simply looked out and saw far, far. Tlingit artist Doug Smarch from Teslin, Yukon, tells the story. It comes from before the Alaska Highway came through. Before US government roadmakers laid down an industrial, hard-packed line over the land.[1]

Smarch tells the story as a frame for his art installation. It begins with a man's search for a lost relation. A medicine man puts the searching man's spirit into a fox, allowing him to travel more easily. After all, this has always has been a place of long walks and great traverses across rigorous terrain. Ease of travel is valuable. In any case what's lost is, in this story, found—the fox covers a distance; relations reunite.

But that is not really where the story is going. On the fox's way home, as he drops down toward his community from the last high hill outside of it, he sees a cloud hanging over his people's dwellings. It is a vision of consequence, and he knows it. When he moves from the fox's body back into his human form, he announces that life is going to change for the Teslin people.

Indeed, he saw far, far.

I wonder if the cloud hung like a pall over the community, or if it hung more as a fine and mystical sweat. Perhaps it moved as other clouds through the restless air or hung as still as the land itself; perhaps it appeared bright in grays and

1. Smarch tells the story publicly, as an artist addressing viewers. Journalists reported on his project a couple years ago. I comb through news archives.

whites, or deep with the bruised greens and purples of electrical storms. I know none of this. I wasn't there. In a magazine interview, Smarch reflects on the fox's vision of change. "It is a beautiful dream," he says, "but it is equally puzzling and disturbing."

Smarch, asking layers of his own questions about the story, makes a feather screen onto and through which he projects digitized images. "Lucinations," he calls the project. The screen hangs like a curtain nearly ceiling to floor, receiving projected beams of light, images from the era when the story's vision of change was to have occurred. The feather screen provides a textured and necessary surface for images to land on, images as liable to create narrative as to unravel it.

The art exhibit was several years ago. I missed it entirely. But people mention it to me with strange frequency. *White lights bobbing on feathers*, they say, jostling their hands in the air. *Maybe you can find a photograph.*

Bundled against the wet spring chill, stepping through lakeside snow, through muck where the snow has melted, and tiptoeing where beached lake ice holds strong and slick, I listen to rolling swan sounds. Perhaps I can warm myself in the warbling blanket of gentle bugling French horn -sounding trumpeters. And so I listen to everything they say, from the bickering to the flirting to the expounding. I have no idea what's what. I simply listen to migrating swans because the world's change is too much when the too-soon spring comes in wet and early and good solid ground goes to soup. There's something soothing in their ancient and wise sounds rolling out across the changing land.

Maybe that is why Smarch turns to so many white feathers. They create a patterned structure. Perhaps he sought texture above all else, texture and repetition, to think through the mist of that historic omen, to summon the fox's vision of change.

The image—those white lights bobbing up and down on a screen of white feathers—it tells another story from Smarch's community, a more recent one. Those white lights bobbing on a screen of feathers illustrate the night that the fox's vision of change came to fruition. It happened like this. One night, the people of Teslin saw lights just like the ones Smarch projects onto the feather screen. They saw round white lights bobbing in the dark far up on the side of the hill far off across the river.

Across the river, or across the bay? Aie, I'm not sure where the people camped that night. I don't know across what part of the water they watched those lights. I'm outside the story.

What I've gleaned is really just about the lights themselves: bobbing lights, far off, across the water, up on the slope of the high hill beyond Teslin. The people of Teslin would have watched those lights through the trees all night. They would have watched those bobbing white lights, wondering what they were, what they foretold. That is how I understand it.

The next day, a government work crew dropped down the hill and out of the boreal forest to the lakeside. They were not the neighboring Southern Tutchone people, or the neighboring Tagish people, or anyone else the Teslin Tlingit usually met, hosted, and traded with. They were the US military. They were roadmakers. A construction crew, or perhaps surveyors trailblazing the route a few days ahead of the main work crew. In any case, it was World War II, Canada and the US were allies, and politicians from Ottawa and Washington, DC, had agreed that Americans would build a road through six hundred miles of northern British Columbia into Yukon and continue another 575 miles to the Alaska border, ultimately linking interior Alaska to the North American continent's road system. Good for war supply transport and such. Good for cooperative allyship between nations in their stand against the "axis of evil." Anyway, Teslin was there, along the way.

So that land—already filled with trade routes, travel ways, and game trails—was to receive one long, sinuous line of pavement across the whole of it. That road came down the hill straight into Teslin. That is how Teslin became a community with a road running through it, and that is, in Teslin, how things have been ever since.

Sites all along the road swelled with inmigrating people. They brought their buildings, institutions, customs, and laws. When white people really put down roots in Yukon, it was with the road that they did it.

Which is to say that the road created the problems I study. It also supports my study of those problems with ease of travel.

The road brought the boreal forest's third colonial inmigration, not its first—that came in the eighteenth century with small parties of far-flung fur traders casting about. The second came with the Klondike Gold Rush of 1898. Each wave brought sudden change. Each put strange pressure on the land and the people living on it. But neither of those first two waves left many permanent new residents. It was the third wave, the inmigration that followed road construction, that marks the pivot. The road changed things across all of Yukon in ways that haven't changed back.

In Teslin, that all starts with a fox's vision of change. His vision is consummated with white lights bobbing far off on the hillside and a night spent with eyes narrowed, watchful of those distant, inexplicable lights.

Navigation systems continue to course through the veins of the earth as they always have. Navigation systems course through all living bodies, from the threads branching through leaves of plants to the bunching alveoli of lungs to continent-wide watersheds sweeping stone into alluvial dust every day. The road came through hard and fast, and I guess all the veins of the earth made an uneasy peace with it. They found a restless cohabitation with that cut through the forest. Incorporated it, if you will. Incorporated it so that now, we all—all of us—people, moose, ptarmigans, fireweed, elk, lynx, ravens, crowberries, grizzlies, rainfall, permafrost, all of us, visitors included, live with it. Yes, that's exactly what we do. We live with it.

But living in a boreal forest with a road cutting through it does not mean we take that road for granted. That is why Smarch creates a work of art that says it straight, speaks to the road's past and present, laying bare its strange and sudden force.

I listen to the voices of eighty-five swans rolling along the lake surface, snowballing into a kind of swan coziness, an auditory swan comforter, and I wonder, thinking back, if there was also a music to the making of the road. Felling of trees, scraping of earth, exploding of quarries, crushing of rock, dumping of gravel, groaning of trucks, cranking of machines—crack of gunshots as construction workers went out hunting in these wild northern lands—hollering of English-language speakers, and nightly, the bending blues of a harmonica and a fiddle and all the other instruments of all the songs sung by workers laboring so very, very far from home. A long, slow (and at once, lightning fast) curl of sound must have unrolled in a thin band as a deafening bolt right across the whole land. Two years it took to build the Alaska-Canada Highway. Hardly time for much silence.

And so I calculate that two years of an utterly unprecedented music, the sound of a road's making, would have unrolled inch by inch through the boreal forest of the Kaska Dena, the Teslin Tlingit, the Carcross/Tagish, the Ta'an Kwäch'än, the Champagne and Aishihik, the Kluane, and the White River peoples.

"Tired yet?" asks a swan sign. *Yes*, I answer. *Yes, I am*. "It's too bad there isn't a nice bench here so you can sit and rest," the sign continues. "Swans experience the same problem as they fly north. Even though they may be tired, if there is no open water, they can't stop for a rest. They have to keep going until they find the right spot."

It is part and parcel of this land: Things move through it. Mastodons at one time, semis at another. I hold my breath, I shut my eyes. Hear what's passing overhead, underfoot. There is movement of course in all things. Even if it is just the rippling soundwaves of a traveler's song from another century, sound keeps dispersing. So I imagine soundwaves as memory following the warp and weft of some weave, traveling forever along a fabric we can only take for what it is, cutting and then sewing it, fashioning it as we can first into shelter, second into warmth. Third into beauty, into thought.

For my part, I wonder if the wheeling cycle of migratory swans can help me see other cycles, transcend my perspective of linearity and loss. Might wartime roadmaking be a dot along the great arc of a wheeling cycle all its own, something that came—and that will, in time, go? A slower story than the ones we live in?

Yes, it might. But I cannot always convince myself of a larger continuity. It is different, the cyclic arrival and sweep of the swans, the repeating seasons, a people's births and deaths and the continuations of kinships across them—all this is different from the steamrolling entrance of a road, fumes emanating from fresh pavement. Different from its firm establishment. Different from the economy of cement that forces seminomadic communities to fixed locations and into fixed configurations of distance and proximity. It is different, the continual life cycle of a swan, from that first road's continual, ruthless begetting of further roads.

Still my stubbornness and I walk the lakeshore, interpretive sign to interpretive sign. "You can rest here," reads the sixth or seventh sign, "but only if no one else is around. If someone else wants to be here, you'll have to move out of the way. The swans feel the same way when people get too close. Just when they find a place to rest, they have to fly or swim away." Wingbeats, incidentally, make the single music for which swans pause their singing. It is the pounding for which even swans have no language. When it is time to fly, swans swallow their words and play the lake like a drum.

A red plastic Adirondack chair tilts in the silt and gravel beach of the lakeside next to the last interpretive swan sign. A chair to assert the stopping place in the most welcoming possible way, a chair hauled out by goodness knows who—Swan Haven caretakers? Yukon government wildlife project managers? Program volunteers?

Maybe a story, like a swan, is something to study carefully—but from afar. Maybe a story is like a creature that ultimately deserves, above all else, its own space. "It's important that you do not go any further than this point," reads the sign, "so that you don't disturb them."

Undisturbed, the swans are busy. They jab their heads into the water, scoop around in the lake muck with their broad, black bills. Come up for air. Add their voices to a hundred others.

Well, there is a chair, and I've arrived, so I sit. The red plastic is quite cold. Mid-April, or is it yet May by the time I am making regular trips out to hear what the swans have to say. The spring air is quite cold; the wind too; the sun bright. Its light almost warms me, and I feel lines of light and shade between almost-warm and certainly-cold crisscrossing my body. I grind the legs of the red plastic Adirondack chair a bit more firmly into the lakeside grit, close my eyes, feel sun on my lids.

When I tilt my head just right, I almost feel the cool shadow cast by my eyelashes onto my cheekbones.

So it is that the body shifts out of eyesight, heightens its hold on the other senses. I can listen more closely now, even as my body tenses against the chill. Can I hear underneath the swans' voices; can I listen for the generations of swans mapping spring in southern Yukon's boreal forest year upon year upon year? Perhaps I can. Brush of air, slice and curve of wing, the turning of centuries. Listen for the cloak of feathers entering and exiting the old stories like the white curtain on which memory depends. Listen to a floating, flapping, pleasantly muck-scooping brass section gone French hornly gentle, a brass section ruffling its fine white feathers, each perfect swan happy to munch on frozen lake muck alongside its regal mate of equally perfect swanness.

But after all this, the sound I settle on—the swan sound that speaks to the center of me—comes not from their voices at all. Not from what they have to say. Nor even how they say it.

In the end, the swan sound that cleaves society's small failures is the drumbeat of their broad white wings pounding the skyward face of the lake when a pair rises to leave it. *Boom, boom; boom, boom.* Swans taking flight reach their broad feather tips as wide as budding tree limbs. Their strong black legs pump the water till their webbed feet break the surface, batting the water to a froth, then tucking into the air, wingbeats pounding the lake all the while. The sound is force. It is muscle. It is speed and angle and determination and precision and heft.

I sit in the red plastic Adirondack chair and feel that old drumbeat in the meat of my heart. Then, and always then, there is the drumbeat's too-soon drop into silence as, in tandem, always in tandem, another pair of swans meets with the sky, joins with the air, two white shapes not jostling but gliding, not descending but rising, not barreling down the hill at anyone's future, not at all. Simply receding, and receding, opening the pale sky into deeper and deeper relief overhead.

PART TWO

The Story of the Day

ATLIN

The salmon runs were weak and the berries got no rain.

—A friend's summary of 2018

The gun cracks and the dog makes a strange move. She is already standing and maybe she will bolt. Two steps and I have her neck skin in my fist; one breath and I have a voice, low and coaxing. *You stay, my friend. You stay.* The shot made everything behind my sternum go hard like sudden lake ice. What's locked in—leaves, pine needles, crushed bubbles—is locked in for good.

The dog doesn't bolt and I loosen my grip, but she could still rocket off the edge of the porch. It's a porch pressed into the edge of the forest in Atlin, British Columbia, just thirty miles south of the Yukon-British Columbia border, an honorary Yukon community. The forest goes for miles until the mountains are too cold for trees, and everything becomes rock and air, air and rock. Then only air. It's country that belongs to highbush cranberries and white spruce, to the T'aaku Kwáan, to moose and grouse. I'm here on a week-long retreat and today a gunshot turned my sternum to ice but I can't freeze; I have to keep hold of the dog. The dog and I hike Monarch Mountain every day but neither of us should beeline out onto the land alone.

Now a truck's tires on gravel, a cut engine. Someone drove up like they know the place. Like they've been here before. From my rented cabin porch I watch cops approach the main house like military men come to tell a woman she's a widow now or that her son is dead. I see heads from beefy shoulders bowed with officialdom. Meaty hands clasped in front of belt buckles. They step away from the door as she opens it, already backing down the front steps as she emerges.

But it's not bereavement they're here to announce and I'm not witnessing a woman's shocked passage from life before loss to life after it. It's the cops they call "conservation officers" and what I see in the woman looks like a testy satisfaction.

Conservation officers patrol Atlin on rotation from Vancouver. They are out on their first two-week assignment some eight hundred miles north of everything they know, deep in the boreal forest at the edge of a stormy lake, a lake from which a single dirt road runs due north joining the community not to any southern city but to Yukon, a lake daily frothed and pounded by the winds racing off glaciers from the Juneau Icefield.

Atlin lies, incidentally, at the inland edge of the very same icefield that oversaw my coastal childhood.

The woman from the main house joins the conservation officers. She hurries down the porch steps and looks once—quickly—into the bed of the truck. The conservation officers exchange cursory comments with her. They all agree: It had to be done.

"Had to."

I rise. I put the dog in. Then I step off the porch. When I approach the conservation officers' truck, when I ask and receive permission to step up on the truck's back bumper, I place my hands as best I can between spatters of blood on the tailgate. I swing myself up and am immediately—according to my whole body—too close to the head of a grizzly bear, her wide and perfect forehead, golden eyelashes ringing her small eyes, fur short and smooth and brown down her muzzle, black lips just parted.

I swear she is still breathing. In the inches between us, my whole body swears she is still breathing.

Even if it's the September wind that moves her coat, an easy brown, golden guard hairs uncanny with warmth in the low-angle light—even if the September wind is what's moving and the light is what's warm and the conservation officers shot her just minutes ago—I swear she is breathing.

She is on her back, head to the right, forelegs bent, wrists relaxed at just the angle Michelangelo painted in his forever present-tense "Creation of Adam" on the ceiling of the Sistine Chapel.

I'm saying the bear's wrists are loosely bent, like yours and mine. Like Adam's when he receives the touch of life.

Shot minutes ago, the bear is still warm, easy, filled with cells that must still be alive. It takes time for life to leave the body. Her eyes are still clear. Her claws are strong and smooth and curved. My whole body knows I am too close. Her blood is bright and there is very little of it, barely pooling beneath her neck. My whole body knows she is breathing, knows she will blink, judge me, and be correct: My presence is wrong. It ought not be me hovering close enough to touch. It ought to be—a god, whatever Michelangelo with his brilliant eye would have meant by that.

That is why I step off the tailgate back down to planet Earth. I am ashamed. Ashamed that I entered this moment.

Though I will say that when I step down my legs have gone clumsy with the dim desire to do exactly the opposite, to crawl into the bed of the truck and lie with her, press my torso to hers in sorrow, in comfort. I want to take the coarseness of her fur on my face without flinching, feel it on my chapped lips, against my windburned cheeks. I want to connect, so that I can breathe so deeply into my belly that her own rib cage begins to move with mine. I want us to expand together, drawing the sky into our dark centers on either side of the warmth between us. I want our bellies to relax in tandem, our lungs to deflate. And then expand again. Forever. That is what I want.

The conservation officers are men in their twenties. I am standing next to them. Men. Out on assignment. They say she probably had a kill, refused to leave it. They say they gave her twenty minutes or so to move on out; she didn't go. Decided twenty minutes was enough, didn't want to wait for an incident, shot her for being there. Shot her for feeding.

I keep hearing it's been a bad year for bears in town. Maybe that's what the conservation officers heard too.

Look.

The salmon runs were weak and the berries had no rain. That is the truth. Her wrists are relaxed like Adam's to receive the touch of life in the September wind.

PERMAFROST IS AN ARCHIVE

I. THE FIELD TRIP

There is a landslide in progress. We're walking on it.

We are a hodgepodge of Yukon University staff and faculty out for a field trip with the Permafrost Lab. They are eager to share their latest find: a drop-shaped permafrost retrogressive toe slump.

The land is sliding away from the road and into the river, explain the scientists. We are walking on it as it goes. But we are not afraid. It is April. Everything is still frozen by the blessed pause that a subarctic winter places on large-scale melting trends. As the scientists put it, *The land is sliding so slowly that it is safe to walk on!* As if "safety" was tangible, real, an actual feature of our world.

The Permafrost Lab director, Fabrice Calmels, holds doubleness as a given: *The ground is hard but be careful. It can be slippy*, he says.

The land may be frozen but the permafrost scientists are right. We can see it going, giving way. We find a basketball-sized hole in the forest floor for example, an early sign that we're on unstable ground. We find another hole here, several over there. Then a few smaller ones, more grapefruit-sized.

Collapses like these are a kind of fortune-telling. They tell us the area is melting. So it is that when land falls out from under itself—underground, that is—surface tears appear, then surface tears multiply. One could say that miniature slumps like these are a kind of overture. They are one way the land announces what's to come.

Now we are all on personal scavenger hunts for holes in the ground. We want space to look at the revealed inches of the underground. We want to put our hands inside holes where needles of ice fill the peaty soil. We spread out like children all wanting to find a floor hole of our own.

Now I'm kneeling in the moss with exactly that, a forest floor hole of my own. My fingers want to touch what I'm seeing. Normal, I suppose. The body tastes its world. Exposed needles of underground ice meet my fingers with the smallest bite of cold, and that sharpness on my skin says I've broken something. My body gives off heat; the earth stings in defense.

Still I run my fingers along the inside of the hole, skimming exposed root threads of Labrador tea, of mosses, of wiry bushes I can't identify. Maybe some of these rootlets even come and go from the spindly black spruce rising around us as forest. Maybe some are hair-thin strands of mycelia connecting the whole community in a fine subarctic, subterranean lattice. What am I doing? Reaching out to touch—what? Interdependence itself?

■ ■ ■

Ten or twelve of us answered the field trip invitation and signed up to ride out in a college van. We drove about an hour west of Whitehorse on the Alcan, the road that crosses northwestern Canada and ties Alaska to North America's continental road system. The US military built the Alcan in tumultuous times—a World War II project—but now the road is a fixture, a piece of inherited furniture, a strip of frost-heaved pavement peeling through hundreds of miles of boreal forest.

On our way to the landslide we hurled down that road, that casual road, the one that in the 1940s changed everything. The spruce forest peeled off the van's bow into a widening *V* in the rearview mirror. We scanned the forest fringe for moose, for lynx; we chatted with our seatmates; then down the van's center aisle came a cardboard box of fluorescent vests.

Row by row, we pulled on tunics of one-size-fits-all fluorescence. Some vests were yellow with white piping. Others were made of orange mesh and rimmed with yellow bands. Seatmates dressed one another and giggled. The van jostled, rocketing over frost heaves.

Pink flagging marks the spot on the road, though a casual driver would not notice the little neon knots on a couple of bobbing willow branches. But we do—that is, the permafrost scientists do. Here we stop. Here we park. We've braked hard on a nearly empty highway, tilted the van halfway off the shoulder into a ditch in the wilderness, killed the engine, added matching hardhats to our fluorescent tunic attire, and walked into the boreal forest with canisters of pepper spray. We're here to see a landslide. Meet it in person.

Why is there a landslide? Melting permafrost. Layers of earth, long frozen as loamy-peaty-icy underground bedrocks—warm, melt, and disintegrate.

Permafrost is, of course, receding everywhere. The globe that hatched blue-green algae that hatched ancient horses that hatched astronauts and poets alike, right now, in the generation-plus that is my whole life: that globe is warming, its waters are acidifying, and its atmosphere is thickening. Over morning coffee, I hear on the CBC's climate report that sensors plunged fifteen feet deep into the earth's permafrost tell us we're warmer than any time in the last fourteen thousand years.

Here in Yukon's Southern Lakes Region, *melting permafrost* means there are places where the underground goes to mush, where ice that's been integrated in the soil for millennia now melts to water. If it's on a slope, then water seeps and percolates and goes downhill, leaving the loamy-peaty soil uphill empty of its old ice structure, free of its old ice scaffolding, weak without the expansive cold clasping of ice crystals. As the ice in the earth melts and runs out, land that was once held up by ice is no longer held up. It falls down. It sinks. It slumps. Seeping meltwater makes a muddy subterranean mess and eventually the top caves in and it all goes downhill. Gravity, and so on. Trees ride it out if they can. Otherwise they snap and fall, sliding in a tangle of trunks.

I know melting is a softening, yet I cannot help but think of it as a brittleness that has come into the bones of the earth's structure. Hard or soft, the structure underfoot breaks down, bit by bit, I know, I know. But it's still what we rely on to hold us up.

And so we take a fieldtrip with the Permafrost Lab and the scientists lead us off the shoulder of the road into the steep roadside ditch and into the forest so we can try to make sense of all this, of the slow-motion, high-speed collapse occurring beneath our hiking-booted feet, of the large-scale melt surrounding life itself, of the still-undeniable feeling the earth is the one thing that offers sure footing.

■ ■ ■

A bird's-eye view.

In the much-farther-than-here far north, the underground is permanently frozen. Permafrost underlies everything. In regions of continuous permafrost, the overall depth of the permafrost layer is shrinking. Change at the earth's surface, where humans thrive, is subtle in this context—the ground still seems stable. We know it's not, but it still feels like it is.

South of here—or close by on the coast where I was born and the climate is temperate—there is no permanently frozen ground; no permafrost. Its melting occurs in the general "elsewhere."

But southern Yukon, *right here*, is a place of transition, of doubleness. It is a land of "discontinuous permafrost."

In regions of discontinuous permafrost some of the underground stays frozen year-round and has been that way for years and years—centuries—millennia—as permafrost. Other parts of the underground freeze and thaw with the seasons. These two kinds of underground clasp one other in a patchwork of subterranean puzzle pieces. Edges press against edges. What's sturdy and frozen lives alongside what's seasonally rhythmic.

In areas of discontinuous permafrost, change at the earth's surface, where humans thrive, is stark.

■ ■ ■

In southern Yukon, as in the rest of the universe, we can usually only see what's above ground. That's just the kind of animal we are. A kind that lives largely on surfaces. A kind in awe of what's beneath. Where the earth begins slowly to collapse, we are astonished by what's inside.

The boreal forest—I wonder what it thinks, if it laughs a little, if it even notices a field trip like this at all. People have lived in these forested mountains for millennia. In fact, people lived here even before the forest did; people lived here when Yukon was a subarctic savannah, an Ice Age tundra. After a time, trees came into the land. Warming, moisture, and so on. So the forest marched north. In any case, it's been home to people the whole time. It's always known us. And so I wonder what it thinks. Here. Today. Of us, fluorescently garbed, peering into surface tears, reaching into holes to touch pins and needles of ice, wiping pale peaty dirt from our hands, awkward in our hard hats.

No time passes at all and now we must carry on. The scientists are excited. *The landslide's center is so close! Just wait!* they say, stepping lightly across the steep terrain and moving with special ease over the springy sphagnum mosses tangled with Labrador tea. *It's a textbook perfect drop shape*, the scientists assure us, *a typical permafrost retrogressive toe slump!*

Typical, as I understand it, means gorgeous.

Or more precisely, it means artful. It means the thing at hand will hit a nerve whether you know what you're looking at or not. Like a curve made of points from the golden mean, like Michelangelo's *David*, like totem poles on Haida Gwaii.

Oh! Here it is! The hillside is quite steep. We cling to branches here and there as needed. And we seem to have arrived at a hole in the forest, not at all basketball-sized but rather a whole basketball court's worth of collapse, a whole long oblong hole where the forest just—sank—sank into a pit eight or ten or fifteen feet deep, sank and slid a ways down the steep hill, trees toppling into a messy jumble and piled up down there, leaving stripped bare an exposed six-foot vertical wall of underground ice up here.

Permafrost, in general, can be as thick as eighty feet. I try to imagine this exposed face at twelve-and-a-half times the scale and catch myself looking up into the sky. Odd, how persistently the direction "down," or the region "underground," slips my imagination.

The scientists love to see our faces. They are eager for our group to climb down into the slump. *Here is the easy way down and into it!* They are poised to hold our hands as we step and hop; they steady us as we find new footing on inside-out earth.

Once we've all scooted-step-hopped down into the hole, they are eager for us to clamber toward the uphill edge of it. *This narrow path of frozen dirt is very stable!* Again, they offer hands. Again, we clamber.

And they are eager for us to go straight up to the curving wall of ice along the uphill curve of the slump. *It's okay to touch! It's very frozen! It will not fall again till June! Maybe July!*

Inside the hole, facing the uphill exposed face away from which all this material slumped and slid downhill, we can see how ice holds the land together. Patterns of sediment mixed with ice. Almost paisley. Swirls of clay, sand, and peat, all mixed in various ways with what looks like cold, dark glass.

What's more, surface water recently spilled over the edge of the forest floor, cascading in a curtain over the cross section of exposed permafrost. It's frozen now—April, remember—and its solid waterfall drapes across one section of curving permafrost. We can walk along the wall of ancient ice; we can pass behind the curtain. The passage is narrow, but in single file, here we are. Left hand on Quaternary permafrost, right hand on this season's silent cascade.

Dirt crunches with ancient ice underfoot, crumbles in steep places where our boots skid. The ground is hard but it can be slippy. We must be careful. We are wearing hardhats and fluorescent vests. I believe now we've simply dressed in such a way so as to remind ourselves that we live in breakable bodies, bodies that can be misplaced and lost in land that is big and deep. Likely bigger and deeper than we have time to understand.

I watch my companions and see that we cannot touch these ancient frozen sediments slowly enough. We cannot touch these black lenses of ancient ice slowly enough. We cannot move our eyes slowly enough to see what we are seeing. The ice is so cold. Hands pressed to the ice fall away one by one. The earth burns us just as we think we are about to register the feel of it. We blow on our fingers, press them against our bellies, try again. But we are people. We are not the kind of animal that can ever do anything slowly enough.

At first, a lake, says one of the scientists. The others nod, pensive. They know we're in and on an ancient lake bed because sediments are legible. These colors, these textures, this is lake bottom grit. Look at the swerves and curls. Look at the blocks, the trapezoids. There was a lake, sediments settling layer by layer on the lake bed, and then there was *maybe some creep*. We must cast aside our images of a placid pond because they mean some restlessness or other pushed the lake bottom into a frenzy. *Layers deformed*. Because look carefully: The sediments are wrinkled, disturbed.

The ice though—it is clear. Horizontal lenses of sheer, black, unbent ice. Straight white pinpricks of stretched air bubbles trapped inside. Silent and full of conviction, of purpose, a stark contrast to the contorted sediments.

And so the scientists know that though the land twisted furiously, one day, it grew calm. And that is when ice came into its depths. *Ice developed after*, they assure us, *ice developed after.* They know because the ice is not convoluted like the sediment. They know because we are looking at ice lenses, perfectly horizontal ice lenses, some as clear and thick as twelve inches. They hold the land together. They clasp the former confusion of the lake bed, remembering it, and holding it on pause in a vast moment of stillness.

When I see sand caught in water, all of it so slick and frozen and perfectly patterned, swirled in exact repetitions—when I see this, I wonder if someone somewhere is already out there dancing their medicine. I wonder if someone's already making a new world, if there is a trick that's already played out. Or maybe the scheming has only just begun. And I wonder if, in the end, and all caprice aside, we'll end up with what we need—I wonder if, in the end, there will be something for us land animals to stand on.

Sand ice will melt faster than clay ice, say the scientists.

We nod, we nod *ah*, we nod *yes*. Sand ice will melt faster. Clay ice will melt slower. *Ah yes*, we nod. And under the forest is the memory of a lake, and in the memory of the lake is the time of sediment deposition, and inside the sediment is cold recollection of this land's convulsions. And later came the ice. And it has all held still a long, long time since then. This year, it rouses.

It's begun to melt, and so it has begun to slide, and we have come to see it in April because it is frozen, and so we are safe; the ground is hard but can be slippy, hence the hardhats. But it cannot collapse all around us until the spring thaws arrive, and so we must tell no one where we are, because this place will be dangerous in the summer.

The road, some distance upslope from us, hasn't collapsed yet, and it'll be a few years till it does. Because the land, melting, falls away. And it falls downhill, away from the road and into the river. Engineers somewhere must be busy, because the part of the road where we parked will, eventually, go with gravity.

Inside the typical, retrogressive toe slump, I keep putting my hand on the ice of the inside of the earth as if I could hold it there, hold something in place, keep one single thing safe in this world long enough to really listen to it, hear it out. Hear it all, all the way out.

II. THE CORE SAMPLES

Fabrice Calmels has ideas about art. He has created, to our knowledge, the world's first public permafrost displays; he is the first to figure out how to store permafrost core samples as an installation. He's placed an array of permafrost cores in glass cylinders of silicone oil and set them in rows inside an upright freezer. The kind they have in liquor stores, with wire racks and glass doors.

One display is in Ottawa, Canada's capital. And one is in the entry of the Permafrost Lab in Whitehorse, Yukon.

As we pile back into the van and finish the field trip, Fabrice learns I am a writer. Or at least he sees that I write things down. Because I am a writer, Fabrice gives me a word. He is theatrical in his delivery. *There's a word for you!* he says. I laugh. *There's a word for you!* he says again, and I've already forgotten it, and he gives me another, cryo-something, and he finds this one so delicious he gets all shivery. *Ooh la la*, he says, ice-language on his tongue. But I am laughing too much and do not write any of it down. "Cryo-something" is all I have to show for it later. That and a fizzled attempt in my notebook at summoning the memory:

Ice suffrage—no
Ice solitude—no
Cryo-something. Some word with an s.

In and among his word giving, Fabrice says I must visit his lab. It is two parking lots away from the Yukon Arts Centre. I wonder how many visitors would, like me, leap at the chance to see an art installation devised by a permafrost scientist.

An art installation: something intended to arrest onlookers and passersby. Intended to render people pensive.

A few weeks later, I meet Fabrice and we go to the Permafrost Lab. Here indeed is an upright freezer with a glass door, lit bright and white from the inside and shelved with white wire racks. Foot-high cylinders stand in neat rows along the shelves. The cylinders are clear and have an oversized test-tube look to them: clean, focused science, they seem to say. In each one sits an ice core in clear liquid, food-grade silicone oil, which does not freeze and distort our vision—but instead gives us a perfectly clear view of each core. Beneath each core is a paper label folded and hung on the wire rack to specify the core's place of origin. *Old Crow, YT Ski Lodge. Alaska Highway, YT km 1896. Jean Marie River, NWT.* And so on.

The Jean Marie River permafrost core is nearly black, loamy in its rich darkness. Others hold all the browns and rusts of muskegs, peat bogs. The sample from Old Crow's ski lodge has pebbles suspended in mud-looking ice like earthly exoskeletons in amber. Others hold fossilized shells, unmistakable signs of ancient seafloors. The blackest, darkest core sample contains near-translucent snail shells, ethereal and terrible all at once. A sample from along the Alaska Highway at kilometer 1738 contains four clear layers: ice, dirt, ice, dirt. In the ice are compressed air bubbles, some needle-stretched and some crushed to a fine lace. The old air an unmistakable sign that someone once used to breathe in there. The earth itself, at least.

I am sure, looking back, that the cryo- word Fabrice gave me must have simply been "cryostructure." As in, *cryostructure can be parallel*—Fabrice's comment about the Alaska Highway km

1738 sample. And *cryostructure can be wavy*—as it is in the gravel from Old Crow. The line "cryo-something, something with an *s*" was just a placeholder in my notes.

Yet I'm dissatisfied with "cryostructure." I do not feel Fabrice's delight in the word. Perhaps the truth is that I've moved on from thinking of ice simply as structure. Scanning for *s* words, I first thought of *suffrage*, remember. Then of *solitude*. Of lone ice casting its one vote. Which, come to think of it, brings *ice sovereignty* to mind.

■ ■ ■

The Quaternary Period is the time of glaciation, best known for the pulsing of glacial periods and global, glacial swings. The Quaternary Period is also the geologic chapter during which humans appeared and proliferated.

All of our sampled permafrost, incidentally, is Quaternary. You can think of permafrost as a feature with human kinship, then, though Fabrice does not use exactly this word. I think he says *related*. Or *together*. As in, *humans and permafrost, we come together into the land*.

I try it out for myself: Humans and permafrost, we come together into the land.

Yes, it is possible. That may be exactly what he said.

Permafrost is an archive. Each permafrost core sample is an archive of thousands of years' worth of atmospheric sampling, geologic sampling, yes, yes. But Fabrice's point is social. Permafrost is an archive of all humanity's time on earth.

In North America, this continent's oldest permafrost is 750,000 years old. *Nearly a million years old!* says Fabrice, asking in the same breath, *but is there older in Russia*? Scientists can be like that, throwing their minds to the horizon. But in my notes his question is just parenthetical, a curio held between the crescents of my shorthand.

Fabrice wants a soapstone carver to work with permafrost cores. *I want a carver to sculpt them in winter*, he says. *We'll display them in freezers in silicone oil*. The sculptures' design will be up to the carver. Creative control rests with the artist.

Though when pressed, Fabrice says he envisions animals. Animals carved in permafrost.

I think of John Berger again, who declares the carving of a bird is not a symbol of a bird—but rather a translated message. An urgent message translated from something delivered by a real bird.

The layers of symbolism, Fabrice exclaims of his imagined permafrost animals, for the material is ancient. It remembers all of human history. And each sculpture will depend—

completely—on the freezer. Should the freezer shut off, as all things eventually and inevitably do, the animal sculptures will melt, change. Even disappear.

Of course Fabrice wants humans to be among the animals carved in his permafrost cores.

I imagine people and their gestures enacting moments so tender and fierce and obscure we breathe sharply when we see them caught, sculpturally stilled in ice-hardened mud. Landslides progress inside us all the time, it seems.

III. THE MAPS

You cannot, when finding the oldest woolly mammoth, change the story of the day, says Fabrice. Some years have passed since he said this. I am still thinking, though, about what he meant. What he meant for himself—and what those words might mean to me.

For Fabrice, the sciences of the underground spend altogether too much time looking back. Paleontology, archaeology, geology, permafrost—all can be historically oriented fields. But I believe it is the future that compels Fabrice to seek answers below ground.

You cannot, when finding the oldest woolly mammoth, change the story of the day, says Fabrice. *I want to change the story of the day.*

Perhaps he means that science understands woolly mammoths pretty thoroughly. Digging up the oldest one ever would have dramatic value, but Fabrice's point is that it would not reconfigure our knowledge of the species. Finding another woolly mammoth won't alter narratives in urgent need of revision.

He tells me that back in 2003 he runs permafrost samples through a CT scan. And that he is probably the first ever to do this. *When you do that, you can tell gas, ice, sediment*, he says. You can see the distribution of each. You can calculate ratios, and you can do all this without destroying the sample. If a sample comes back 50 percent ice, for example, you know land can slump by 50 percent when it melts.

The really important thing, to Fabrice, is to solve problems. The CT scan permits core analysis *and* preserves the core. It's like Christopher Columbus and the egg, he says. Challenging his critics to stand an egg upright on a table, Columbus solves the riddle himself by cracking the tip of the egg, standing the now-broken egg perfectly upright. *It's easy*, says Fabrice, *but you have to think about it*.

That is how he likes to work: by thinking about it. Using silicone oil to visually display frozen cores—maybe it's easy. Using a CT scan is maybe easy too. *But you have to think about it*, he keeps saying. Meaning you have to think *of* it. And if no one's yet thought of it—maybe it's not so easy.

Take, for example, the Permafrost Lab's hazard mapping. Residents of Jean Marie River (population seventy-seven)[2] in Canada's Northwest Territories said they worried about two things: permafrost and food security. Fabrice wanted to put the two concerns together. And so he did. He believes his Permafrost Lab is the first to create community hazard maps. *Why avoid aligning science problems with social science?* he asks.

Here's an example. Say you're interested in food security. You want to know if the land your people depend on for berry harvests can slump by 50 percent. Because if it does, the vegetation is liable to change. Or say you're interested in infrastructure. Similarly, you want to know if the land beneath the airstrip is liable to slump or if the building site selected for the new school rests on stable ground.

If a community tells the permafrost scientists where their most prized berry patches are, where they run their trap lines, where they go to harvest caribou versus moose versus sheep, what their infrastructure plans look like, then the permafrost scientists can map out that community's uses of surrounding lands. They can overlay the picture with their permafrost studies. They can come back to the community and show them areas that sit on melting permafrost, or down watershed from melting permafrost, and predict when and how those areas will change.

2. At the time of the 2016 census.

Now the halls outside Fabrice's office are filled with colorful, precise, digitally printed posters that integrate permafrost data with community planning issues.

Take palsa formations. A palsa is ice and peat and sediment, layers of each that make a bulge, or a hill. They stipple the boreal forests with added topography. Frozen.

But in this era the world's winters grow scrawny. And summers muscle up, searing the land. Ice caps melt, creating a feedback loop: less global ice means less light-reflection means more light-absorption means more heat absorption means more ice cap melting. Alongside the ice caps, Arctic tundra permafrost melts as well, creating another feedback loop: melting permafrost releases anciently stored methane into the atmosphere, which contributes to the greenhouse effect, which contributes to the warmth melting permafrost in the first place.

A palsa formation is an occasion for the local to take center stage against this global backdrop. When a palsa melts, its bulge on the land collapses, flattening out. The palsa's meltwater . . . well. It does as it can, as water must. It seeps, it percolates, it flows. It moves downhill. Perhaps it swells the local watershed and a rivulet becomes for a few years a significant creek. Or perhaps a melting palsa's water accumulates in a low place, rendering historically dry ground spongy so that tundra lichens drown and thick mosses and shrubby willows move in. Perhaps palsa meltwater gets trapped and even forms a swamp, creates a marsh. Where caribou browsed lichen in past years, perhaps ducks paddle about and moose wade in slowly, soft lips pulling at water plants below and willow buds above.

It's not an apocalypse.

Or maybe it is.

The Greek word for apocalypse—*apokalyptein*—does not mean a catastrophic undoing. It means *uncovering*, the lifting of a veil.

As the land shifts and turns underfoot, let us peer beneath the veil. For myself, I feel strangely galvanized. Standing in the corridor, awash with the maps' colors, I say to Fabrice that I want to learn to read these maps. I *have* to learn to read them. Fabrice claps his hands. *We made them for you!* he says, though he doesn't mean me personally. He means people with little to no training in Western science and engineering. Observant people, pensive people, people who look for and see patterns, connections, tensions, possibility. They are not made for those who would pore over fine print; they are made for people to resee the land they know and have always known. He could have said: Every layer of information on the permafrost hazard maps is an opening. A facet of the art.

You cannot, when finding the oldest woolly mammoth, change the story of the day. But Fabrice, he wants to change the story of the day.

So I think about that.

I think about the day.

Its story.

What Fabrice means when he says he wants to change it.

Maybe I even think about what I might mean, if I were to say such a thing myself.

If.

YFN 101: WHAT WE GIVE TO ONE ANOTHER

I am going to tell you a story about a doorknob. Not a door. Though a door is a good metaphor: It places a threshold between then and now.

As if past and future could be divided.

The story begins with a woman striding up the steps, perhaps a clipboard in hand, perhaps hands nestled into huge down mittens. So far, I am inventing. See her crisp arrival at the top step, barely any pause on the narrow front stoop, a quick rap at the door because almighty it is *cold*, and with that rap the door swings wide on its loose and easy hinges because the doorknob? It is broken and restrains nothing.

The door swings open and pulls a torrent of white winter air deep into the lungs of the house. *Dammit!* The woman lunges for the knob. See her reach, fumble, a slight and bundled body thrown forward to catch the door and pull it back—for the love, pull it back—but the clipboard—or perhaps the huge down mittens—she misses the knob, trips a little, finds herself one step inside someone else's house, though she is most concertedly not trying to break and enter and goddammit why don't these people fix their stupid, stupid doorknobs.

One of my YFN 101 teachers tells us this story. This class is officially "Yukon First Nations 101," but everyone calls it YFN 101. It is a one-day history of Yukon's fourteen First Nations.

So my teacher starts this history by telling us about the stupid, stupid doorknobs. About her clear wash of spite over broken, unfixed doorknobs. And more specifically, her clear wash of spite for the First Nations people who, when the doorknob breaks, just leave it that way.

What I didn't know, she says, *was that for one hundred fifty years they were not allowed to replace the doorknob.*

Of course she was quick and animated as she told the story, and of course she is very quiet now.

They didn't own the house, she says. *They didn't have the right to buy a doorknob.*

The doorknob is literal. It isn't a metaphor. Not yet. Not that I can trace. Of course this worries me. My expectation is that the doorknob is trying to tell us something more, something crucial—I expect the doorknob to crack something open beyond what the story says for itself.

What my teacher didn't know—but now knows and teaches us—is that for 150 years neither First Nations nor Inuit nor Métis people did not, in all of Canada, have the right to buy a doorknob.

You'd have to call the Band Office, she says, voice low.

The band office would have to call Ottawa.

Ottawa would decide what doorknob to buy, who's going to buy it, who's going to pick it up, and when it's going to happen.

For 150 years, for a First Nations person, living in a house with a door, that is what it took to fix a doorknob.

One hundred fifty years, repeats my teacher. *One hundred fifty years.*

That level of dependency, she says. *That level of control. Of* micro *control.*

Again she is quiet. Of course we are too.

And then my teacher takes a breath, rinses the memory down. We're going to move on. We're going to move on, but we are not really going to move on; we are going to circle the thing at hand, come at it from another angle now. She is a good teacher.

First Nations did not ask for this relationship, says my teacher. *The Canadian government asked for this relationship. This is why self-determination is a driver of discourse. . . .*

YFN 101 is required learning for all staff, faculty, and students at Yukon University. Many organizations also require it for their employees, their boards of directors, and their contractors. Everyone, at some point, gets their one-day history of all fourteen First Nations. Everyone takes YFN 101. Everyone.

All of Yukon's fourteen First Nations participated in the course design. And in an astonishing instance of consensus and efficiency, all fourteen First Nations agreed on this curriculum, on the content and design of all printed literature and materials supplied, and on a co-teaching model that always places two voices at the front of the room. From institutions with bad policies to hitches in human interactions, from Yukon and Canada and North America statistics on Indigenous suffering—to a single spiteful doorknob—YFN 101 is the most basic, introductory, essential opening toward reconciliation.

YFN 101 is designed, of course, to be much like stepping through a door.

■ ■ ■

I have a Yukon-based teaching gig with a summer program for journalism majors. It's an intensive course in reconciliation storytelling. Six journalism students traveled from Canada's urban east coast to Whitehorse, where we have a month to coach them on local politics and histories, immerse them in Yukon cultures, and prepare them for ten days of field work in the fly-in community of Old Crow where they'll research, write, photograph, film, and produce their own works of reconciliation journalism. My part: "creative nonfiction bootcamp."

But today, my co-teacher and I are students alongside our students. We've gathered at the Ayamdigut campus of Yukon University in Whitehorse for a full day of YFN 101. It's early summer and the classroom windows are open. We've dispersed around a large horseshoe of desks, filtering in with perhaps twenty or twenty-five others, most of whose seasonal employment requires the class.

Our YFN 101 teachers take turns speaking. Early in the course's introduction, one of them makes an incredible slip. *There's some really challenging stuff in here*, she says of the YFN 101 curriculum. *There's some really challenging stuff that's in our near future—I mean our recent past—*

I am, of course, enthralled. The entire premise of the course is that the past is with us here in the present, and that we should all, every single one of us, get to know it.

So. Here are my day's notes from YFN 101's story of the near-recent future-past.

■ ■ ■

Permanent European settlement in Canada happens in about 1600—because of cod, and because of beavers.

That's the eastern side of the continent, though. Permanent settlement in western Canada happens much later.

A fight for dominance over the fur industry between the British and French produces a seven-year war. The British win; France cedes most of its land to Great Britain.

The British admit they are terrible at forming relationships with Indigenous people. They make laws about this, such as the "common law," in which the British acknowledge they have to negotiate with Indigenous people for the land.

In 1763 a "Royal Proclamation" establishes aboriginal right and title, which recognized that all land would be considered aboriginal land until it is ceded by treaty. What the British want (my teacher specifies) is to be the only ones who can negotiate with Indigenous peoples.

The first formal settlement in western Canada dates to 1849. A British colony is established on Vancouver Island by James Douglas. He buys a bunch of land from First Nations. Joseph

Trutch follows. He reduces First Nations reserve land by 91 percent.

In 1862 a smallpox epidemic sweeps through British Columbia. Between 35 and 60 percent of First Nations people perish.

There are a few fur traders and some missionaries in Yukon at this time. First Nations in Yukon are semi-nomadic, and as one of my teachers put it, *pretty healthy*.

But there are conflicts. Conflicts between Burwash and Beaver Creek. Conflicts with the Tlingit who control the coastal-inland border. Yet Tlingit control of access routes over the Coastal Mountains into Yukon buys Yukon First Nations extra time. This is to say that coastal Tlingit people buffer Yukon's inland peoples. For some generations inland people do not really have to reckon with the settler presence firmly established on the coast.

By the time western Canada is getting settled, Euro-descendants have been in Canada for generations. They migrate into western Canada and settle there with the entitlement that comes with an established sense of being at home in North America.

In 1867 Russia—seeing their Alaskan sea otter fur trade dry up as a function of overhunting, and recognizing that they could not possibly win a war against the British (should Great Britain try to take Alaska by force)—puts Alaska up for sale.

But Great Britain passes it up. Instead it's the US that seals the deal. Critics call the purchase Seward's Folly. Many see the North as useless land. At best an icebox.

Alaska thus shifts imperial hands. No longer Russian, it becomes American. *Well Great Britain,* says my teacher, *they flip their lid.* Because with that purchase, Great Britain sees the US moving into the North. Great Britain sees the US competing with British control of northern North America. Great Britain scrambles to *get their poop in a group*. It solidifies Canada's sovereignty and turns Canada into its own country in the hopes of more firmly establishing control over this enormous region of North America.

That is why 1867 is both the year of the US purchase of Alaska and the year of Canada's founding.

It takes just less than a decade for the newly sovereign country of Canada to pass its Indian Act. That law, passed in 1876, legislates virtually every aspect of First Nations existence. It places Indigenous peoples across Canada under some of the strictest state control imaginable.

Interestingly, Canada's Indian Act is still in effect.

Some examples of the document's highly controlling intentions: Where Indians can live. What they can wear. Where they can hunt. But the Indian Act also delineates the government's fiduciary responsibility to work *with* Indians.

In 1879 Nicholas Flood Davin writes a report recommending Canada follow the US example of residential schools to control and assimilate aboriginal populations. And to disconnect children from families and communities.

In 1884, just five years after the confidential Davin Report is submitted to the Canadian government in Ottawa, we see a big amendment to the Indian Act. The government enacts anti-potlach laws, taking away the right to gather. And the government gives responsibility for the education of aboriginal children to church-run residential schools.

I will be born on the first centennial of this event.

What of my own US side of the border? The anniversaries are not so clear. US missionaries run residential boarding schools with the goal of civilizing and assimilating Indigenous youth as early as the seventeenth century. Outside of class I will scour the internet, add to the margins of my YFN 101 notes. Wikipedia mentions a Jesuit mission established in 1634 in what's now Maryland—that mission declared its purpose to be both civilizing and instructional. Perhaps that makes it a school. Well, 350 years after *that*, I will be born.

In piecing this together I note that it's not always easy trying to meet history eye to eye, as a neighbor from the present. Yet we can't all be historians, we can't sift for clues all day long—so what are we to do in the face of an elusive, essential fact? I appreciate YFN 101 anew. It's organized, a full-day meet and greet with the national past, a lesson in the arts of hosting. Indeed I suppose I feel . . . welcomed. Welcomed into Canada's national imperial history—and by extension North America's imperial history—one I'm walking around in whether I know it or not.

Alaska and Yukon, 1898, an iconic year for the Klondike Gold Rush. Overall, an estimated one hundred thousand prospectors migrate into Yukon from 1896 to 1899, boating and walking through various parts of Alaska to get there.

With a stated objective of assimilation, the author and administrator Duncan Campbell Scott rules (runs?) Canada's Department of Indian Affairs from 1913 to 1932. Later when I check the internet, I find the Canadian Encyclopedia calls Scott "an acclaimed poet" and a "controversial public servant."

A 1920 amendment to the Indian Act alters the definitions of "Indian status." Now, a "Bill C-31 Indian" is an Indigenous person who didn't have status but got status back through this amendment. Indigenous people who did not qualify for Indian status were barred from living on reserves and thus barred from living in their communities. One may then prefer to have status rather than not.

But status was perhaps as much about stripping rights as non-status was. For example, a status Indian could join the

Canadian military, could be sent to war—but upon return, a status Indian soldier would not be awarded veteran status or veteran recognition, resources, or services.

A 1927 amendment to the Indian Act forbids Indians from hiring an attorney for legal consultation. It also forbids legal representation.

For eight months and twelve days of 1942, some thirty thousand US military and civilian personnel build 1,680 miles of the Alaska Highway across British Columbia and Yukon, tying Alaska into North America's road system.

The highway "opens" Yukon, heralding a wave of settler inmigration.

The highway causes fur prices to drop and pulls First Nations away from traditional modes of life on the land.

The highway dramatically increases state access to First Nations children. It becomes much easier for the state to conscript children into residential schools.

Of the road, Elders say, *This is when we lost the territory.*

A 1951 Indian Act amendment removes anti-potlach laws. Gatherings of more than ten First Nations people were illegal; now they are legal.

But section 88 of the 1951 amendment to the Indian Act gives the provinces jurisdiction over Indigenous child welfare where none existed federally. This allows for the Sixties Scoop, a period between the late 1950s and early 1980s when child welfare agencies chose not to provide community resources to Indigenous communities but simply to remove children from their homes.

My teachers are quite clear on this point: First, families lost their children to the residential school system. Then families lost their children to child welfare. All First Nations, Inuit, and Métis communities are shaken to the core.

We don't have a solution, says one of my teachers.

We don't have a solution, but we do need to have a basic relationship with some of the facts. That is why Yukon's fourteen First Nations came together in agreement on this course, its curriculum, its delivery. No, we don't have a solution, and yes, we do need to incorporate history into our sense of today.

A chair creaks. The wind outside our open windows shifts. A page of someone else's notes catches the breeze and rides the air off of a desk and onto the floor. One of my teachers rests her eyes there, on someone's quiet page landing on the carpet. Then she picks it up. Absently places it back on a surface. *Trauma means . . .* she begins. *Trauma means there* are *First Nations Inuit Métis families that are* not *safe for children. But the family unit has been under attack for generations. And the family unit being under attack by Child Services is a problem in every territory and every province of Canada.*

When I first revisit my notes and begin writing this essay, it is 2020 and the US and countries watching us enter a third week of protests against police violence. The Minneapolis police have murdered George Floyd. I think back to YFN 101 and mull over today's emerging slogan, "defund the police." I think of government departments that fail the people, and those that serve the people.

Though Aboriginal title is established in 1867 by royal proclamation, more than a century passes before Canada's federal government recognizes it. The year 1973 marks the moment. A Canadian Supreme Court decision, *Calder v. Attorney General of British Columbia*, recognizes the Aboriginal title of the Nisg̱a'a.

In 1982, with section 35, Canada's Constitutional Act recognizes existing Aboriginal treaty rights. In 1984 Pope John Paul II visits Canada and says, as my teacher paraphrases him, *Canada's Aboriginal people have the right to self-government, their own resources, and their own economy*. The moment is riddled with irony, for Catholic church residential schools have perpetrated generations of physical and sexual violence on their First Nations, Inuit, and Métis students. The pope is nonetheless a public voice. His statement reflects changing times. It introduces new pressure on Canada's government.

Canada's court makes another important legal decision in 1997 with *Delgamuukw v. Her Majesty the Queen*. The Supreme Court rules

> that Aboriginal title has *never* been extinguished,
>
> that the government has to recognize oral history as evidence in court,
>
> that the government has to consult Aboriginal people and compensate them when infringing on their established rights, and finally,
>
> that the Supreme Court confirms title to hunt *and* jurisdictional authority over how land is used.

In 2015 Canada's Truth and Reconciliation Commission—the TRC—releases its six-volume report, including ninety-four "calls to action" to further reconciliation between Canadians and Indigenous peoples.

▪ ▪ ▪

That is Canada's national imperial background as presented by YFN 101 and noted by me.

We've traveled through events from 1600 to 2015, from fur trapping to Truth and Reconciliation. It occurs to me that YFN 101's central achievement is orientation. It's only a very distant cousin to the history seminars I remember from my postsecondary years, seminars full of primary documents and slides and discussion of values and motivations and blind spots. Instead YFN strikes me as closer kin to guided back-country travel. A good guide may show you the way from here to there. But that is only part of it. A good guide will probably share stories, sharpen one or two of your skills, and most crucially, they will set you up for difficulty. And flashes of success. YFN 101 is like that: a supported foray onto fraught terrain. And I think that is key to its purpose. YFN 101 is a history course not for scholars but for society—a guided orientation for us as citizens to take better stock of where we are.

■ ■ ■

Now we home in. With Canada's national imperial history as foundation, we turn to YFN 101's "Yukon Story." I start a new page of notes.

I think I learned to take notes because someone taught me that the hand hears what the ear cannot. I feel there is a truth in this and bend over the page. This is YFN 101's "Yukon Story" as received and reshaped through one hand of my own body.

Three to four generations of Yukon's First Nations peoples went to residential schools.

In the rest of Canada, seven to nine generations of First Nations Inuit Métis went to residential schools.

Some say that healing requires the same number of generations *out* of residential school as were *in* residential school.

Residential schools are replete with patterns of abuse, right? My teachers say no. They describe something else—something I call, in my notes, *patternless*.

My teachers argue the abuse was senseless, as in, something out of which sense cannot be made. (*Meaningless* or *useless* suffering, as Emmanuel Levinas put it after the Holocaust.) Free of pattern, absent of sense: *We know the schools were rampant with abuse by both sexes, perpetrated against both sexes.* That is as far into the big picture as my teachers will go.

They turn instead to the particulars.

Officials took lots of Old Crow students from above the Arctic Circle down to Chooutla, in Carcross. *Too far to send them home for birthday, hey?* says my teacher.

Residential schools were funded by the federal government and each was run by a church (for example, Anglican, Catholic, Baptist). Canada founded and ran 139 residential schools. The local ones are these:

Carcross Indian Residential School—Chooutla—Caribou Crossing

My teacher's mom went here, to Chooutla.

It was open from 1911 to 1969.

Choutla was an Anglican school. Operated for seventy-eight years.

Originally, Choutla opened at Forty Mile near Dawson City. It moved to Whitehorse in 1903, then to Carcross in 1911, burned down in 1939, and was rebuilt in 1953 after the war.

Children did the labor.

Choutla was known for its large gardens.

All that food went to the community of Carcross and to Choutla staff. Students tell stories of hunger.

Saint Paul's Hostel

Operated from 1920 to 1943.

Anglican.

Located in Dawson City.

A school for "half-breed" kids. Not eligible, therefore, to receive government funding. But Choutla didn't allow half-breeds. Hence the need for Saint Paul's.

My teacher says exactly this: *half-breed*. I take notes on history but really I am trying to understand the sucker punch of language. Last century's language in the mouth of my teacher, my teacher whose mother went to Choutla, my teacher who watches the room with her even, even eyes. Doggedly, I take my notes. And I do my best to take them verbatim. I think I do this because I trust her. I trust that there is a lesson inside the language, that she chooses her words wisely and with purpose, that I cannot fully absorb the past, that language will be my landmark—on uncertain ground, along an ambiguous journey.

> *Shingle Point* or *Saint John's*
>
> Located at Shingle Point, Yukon, near Aklavik in Northwest Territory.
>
> Operated from 1929 to 1936.
>
> Anglican.
>
> Used old structures left by the fur trading Hudson's Bay Company.
>
> *An experimental Eskimo boarding school*, or the first residential school created specifically for Inuit children. During the flu epidemic, staff put two to three students in each bed. Contagion thrived.

It happened, says my teacher, *that children died and parents weren't told.*

Nor, often enough, was the government told. So that one hundred dollars per child keeps rolling in from the federal government and it's left on the other children to bear the news when they return home.

Stacking bodies. Hard to tell now whose bones are whose. Schools had not playgrounds but cemeteries.

Because schools willfully kept inaccurate records of children's deaths, and because even archaeologists have trouble accurately counting stacked child bodies in mass child graves, professional estimates vary from 3,600 to 6,000 deaths in Canada's 139 recognized residential schools.

Whitehorse Baptist Mission School

(I've heard a little about this one outside of YFN 101. People say it was founded in no small part to care for bands of roving children. The situation: Parents might come in off the land and into town, desperate for work. Maybe they'd find employment, maybe they wouldn't. Maybe they'd find it but it wouldn't last. Either way, there were years in Whitehorse in which noticeably large bands of children seemed to need food, clothing, and structure. The Mission School was a local answer to this local situation. That is what I heard. My notes though are only two lines long.)

Operated in downtown Whitehorse from 1947
to 1968.
Among its more insidious policies: Children were often
made to punish each other.

Here, says my teacher, *lies the core of lateral violence*. Children returned to communities having betrayed one another. Children returned carrying vendettas.

Yukon Hall

Nondenominational but intended for children from Protestant families.

Operated from 1956 to 1965 in Whitehorse's Riverdale neighborhood.

Now it's just an empty lot down by Christ the King School.

This school, says my teacher. *We get pushback*. She explains: The YFN 101 curriculum gets pushback. People remember being enrolled *past that date*, past the textbook closure date of 1965. We are all furrowed brows and tilted heads. What does an uncertain fact require of a thinker, of a citizen?

Well, after it closed—which could be 1965 but was probably not 1965—after it closed, it was repurposed. The Kwanlin Dün First Nation used the building for council offices. *Yukon leaders abused here had to work here*, says my teacher.

Later, Kwanlin Dün agreed to have the building torn down.

I think I know the place; I ride my bike past there pretty often. Sometimes I see someone at the edge of the empty lot. I know now that when I see someone standing there, they may be waiting for the bus, but they may also be there to think about something.

Whitehorse Hostel or *Coudert Hall*

Catholic.

Across the street from Yukon Hall. Operating during the same period.

This later became the building of the Yukon Native Brotherhood.

Again, begins my teacher. *The resilience of people going back in to a place of abuse to do good work uplifting the community—*

There is long quiet. She is unwilling, it seems, to finish the sentence.

Lower Post

Operated from 1951 to 1975. Catholic.

One of the top-five-worst documented schools in Canada.

Needles through tongues for speaking language.

Eight documented pedophiles on staff.

The Trailblazers come out of here. You know them? The Trailblazers, they start the trials against the abusers. They were the first to step forward. Their court cases occurred *in that school*.

Don't paint every First Nation with the same brush, says my teacher, and quite suddenly. *There were families that went into the bush, there were families that hid their children, there were people who got away.*

There always are, I think. And we must remember, I infer, not to presume we know who's who.

■ ■ ■

YFN 101 arrives from Canadian history through Yukon residential school history to the central facts defining Yukon today: land claims.

The Umbrella Final Agreement (UFA) as an agreement in principle is reached in 1989. It is signed in 1993.

Eleven Yukon First Nations have signed on to the UFA and begun processes of land claims negotiation and self-government negotiations. Three Yukon First Nations have not signed on to the UFA.

For example, the Kaska in Ross River haven't signed. They haven't signed because *they hate giving up their land to get their land*. (My teacher is referring to the Cede, Release, and Surrender clause appearing on page 15 of the ninety-page agreement. Under this clause, a First Nation must first cede its lands to the crown. Only then can they negotiate regaining legal control over some portion of it.)

As another example, White River hasn't signed, either. But for them, it's because half of their people are on the US side of the border and if they negotiate they'll have to exclude Alaskans from the White River Nation.

■ ■ ■

We're nearing the close of a one-day class. There will be a Q and A.

We rustle papers, we breathe. Our peripheral vision sharpens; we remember we are sitting in a large horseshoe elbow to elbow with others. We remember where we are, who we are, and for myself, I remember my own students scattered around the horseshoe of the room. East Coast city kids enrolled in a highly respected school of journalism, traveling in Yukon for five weeks of reconciliation storytelling.

I do not yet know what I feel, but it is possible my students feel submerged. On the other hand, I trust them. They are here out of good will. They care. They want to know. They want to respond to the simple, most unwieldy facts of this world.

A student journalist raises his hand. He asks our YFN 101 teachers how, as a settler, to respectfully enter Indigenous spaces.

Two weeks from now, we will take our journalism students to the fly-in community of Old Crow above the Arctic Circle on the banks of the Porcupine River, traditional territory of the Vuntut Gwitchin Nation. He must be thinking of this. He must be thinking of the room he's sitting in and of the rooms he will enter in the days and weeks to come. He raises his hand. How, he asks, can he—as a settler—enter Indigenous spaces, respectfully.

He wears a light pink shirt and jean cutoffs and tilts his head. His voice is gentle, his legs are crossed in impossibly tight curves, and he is very, very smart. He is legibly and wonderfully queer. These observations are at once the most superficial yet central facts of the moment—what's more, these are my own sightlines—while in truth the moment belongs not to me but to him and to his voice and to his question of Indigenous spaces, his search for how he as a settler can respectfully—

Our teacher leans forward with one hand up. She stops him cold.

It's your space too, she tells him. And with one firm *hm?* she nods once; intent, uninterruptable. *It's your space too*.

Her co-teacher spoke to us of laws preventing her people from fixing doorknobs. Of bones atop bones, the cemeteries of children. She herself spoke to us of her mother who went to Chooutla, a school with a graveyard of its own. And in this moment, with her even gaze and a single upheld hand, she asserts one thing: We're in it together.

It's your space too.

Some years have gone by. If I'm lucky, more will come. For now, here I am, still thinking of what passed between them. When has a full stop ever been so . . . full?

I often take my notes verbatim. It means I miss a lot, don't really track main ideas, and for better or for worse, I set down sentences free of context. In the end, my notebooks are perhaps a better record of rhythms than of information, a collage of turning points over conclusions. Perhaps by documenting exact sentences I simply outline the negative space around what's uttered aloud. Perhaps my real object is to get into the thick of the wordless, to record the unspoken.

I remember the student's pale pink T-shirt. His tilted chin, his crossed legs. His searching eyes—*it's your space too, hm?*, the teacher asserts, unsmiling, hand directing an unequivocal halt. *It's your space too.*

He offers his own erasure; she truncates its very possibility. What's left? Kin. A horizonless ocean.

The earth orbits. The storms surge. The land melts. Solid ground, then, may have more to do with what we give to one another than anything else. What can any of us stand on in the end if not the firm trust one person invests in another?

CHOOUTLA: TRUTH AND RECONCILIATION

Education got us into this.

—Murray Sinclair

I will go to the archives. What will I look for? Another place, simply, where the past speaks?

I call Linda Johnson, former territorial archivist of Yukon. I tell her I am going to the archives. *What should I do there? What should I look at; what should I learn?* Linda's response is prompt. She points me to the archive's residential school records. Choutla's. Why? Because they exist. Because the Anglican church left records.

The Catholic church hasn't shared anything, says Linda. *No records. We have only survivor accounts. They surged in—the Roman Catholics did—with highway construction.*

Anglicans were already around. They were in a real competition for souls. Baptists were around, too. In the forties they founded a school in Whitehorse, the Whitehorse Baptist Mission School. But like northwest Canada's Catholic church–run schools, the Mission School also chose to leave no records.

The only residential school records in Yukon are Anglican church records. At the archives. They went through and destroyed particularly troubling items. But there's still lots there. There are restrictions of course—to protect privacy. So there's lots to see and there's also lots you can't see. But, for example, you can still read church workers' correspondence. There's a fair amount of it. And you can still page through certain clips from the school newspaper.

I will follow Linda's advice. And I will see if old papers and pamphlets speak of the histories among us just as rocks and ice do.

That disconnect between what the church thought it was doing—and what students were experiencing—go there. You'll find parallel universes, never the twain shall cross kind of thing.

■ ■ ■

The archives are well lit. The ceiling is triangular and made of something strong but translucent so that light from the sky, from the world, washes over the research tables. I look at the light overhead and wait for an archives technician to bring me

Chooutla's public records from the stacks downstairs. She arrives and unloads a series of trays, placing them on the table in front of me. There are pamphlets, letters, a couple of books.

She is curious about the materials I requested, materials she's pulled from the stacks and carted upstairs. And so she lingers. We page through documents together for a few minutes.

We talk.

Then she leaves.

And I continue alone. I pause over a brief column printed in the *Weekly Star* on August 27, 1915, titled "Foreman Wood Here." The column reads, in its entirety:

> Jimmie Wood, the Indian boy who has been foreman of the Northern Light office, the Chootla Indian school printing office near Carcross, was here several days this week on his way to his ancestral home at Moosehide where he will engage in teaching other natives the gentle arts of civilization. Jimmie has been a pupil in Carcross school for the past nine years or just half his life, he now being eighteen years of age. Foreman Dech of the Star office gave Jimmie his first lesson at typesetting in the office of the Daily Alaskan in Skagway several years ago since which time the little fellow has become quite proficient at the business. Jimmie may decide to start a paper, the Moosehide Morning Scent, in his own village.

What is behind news like this? The past? Or the future?

I reflect. Those "gentle arts of civilization." Those gentle, genocidal arts. Every day we fumble our way into the unknown, and every day reporters reflect this wayfinding back to us. Jimmie may indeed decide to start a paper, and if he does, he will daily or weekly or on a schedule of his choice do what reporters do: remind us something has happened, that something is in the midst of happening. Now.

Now.

Those gentle arts.

▪ ▪ ▪

The Anglican church ran a school in Carcross, not far from Whitehorse, called the Chooutla Residential School. Chooutla operated from 1911 to 1969. Once it burned down. They rebuilt it then—larger, larger—to account for overcrowding in other schools.

Children from all over Yukon attended Chooutla. Many came from the Vuntut Gwitchin First Nation in Yukon's farthest north community, Old Crow. Others came from Ross River, Kwanlin Dün, Ta'an Kwäch'än, Tagish K̲wáan, Tlingit communities from the West, and more. Some students even came from the Northwest Territories and British Columbia.

In *Finding Our Faces*, a book written by survivors about their experiences at the Whitehorse Indian Mission School (run by the Baptist church), Whitehorse poet Sweeny Scurvey thinks back to the 1940s. He reflects on the region's schools. He recalls Chooutla's reputation. "Dad heard about Carcross, lots of deaths, so he kept us away from there," says Scurvey. In contrast, "When someone came to take us to Whitehorse [Indian Mission School], he okayed it."

Though Scurvey's dad kept him and his siblings out of it, Chooutla's reach was wide. It's said that all of Yukon's First Nations people living today either attended Chooutla themselves or have a family member who did.

■ ■ ■

Education, Tosh Southwick says, *is a space of transformation.*

Tosh is a member of the Kluane First Nation. When I speak to her in 2019, she is Yukon College's (now Yukon University's) newly appointed associate vice president of Indigenous Engagement and Reconciliation. I've come to campus to get her take on Canada's *Truth and Reconciliation Report*—the country's national effort at reckoning with residential school history.

Canada's Truth and Reconciliation Commission (TRC) was active from 2008 to 2015. It was a formal, institutionalized effort resembling South Africa's TRC. Whereas South Africa's

TRC was formed to address apartheid, Canada's was created to inform all Canadians about what happened in residential schools.

Needless to say—or, essential to say?—at the time of this writing, the US has not held a TRC of its own. Neither to address chattel slavery, nor to address genocidal colonialism.

For seven years, Canada's TRC conducted extensive research, compiled meticulous records, and prepared a comprehensive report on the policies and operations of its residential schools and their lasting impacts. The final report included "Ten Principles for Reconciliation" and "94 Calls to Action." These speak in direct address to all sectors of Canadian society.

For example, the first call to action addresses child welfare and looks like this:

> We call upon the federal, provincial, territorial, and Aboriginal governments to commit to reducing the number of Aboriginal children in care by:
>
> (i) Monitoring and assessing neglect investigations.
>
> (ii) Providing adequate resources to enable Aboriginal communities and child-welfare organizations to keep Aboriginal families together.
>
> (iii) Ensuring that social workers and others who conduct child-welfare investigations are properly educated and trained about the history and impacts of residential schools.

(iv) Ensuring that social workers and others who conduct child-welfare investigations are properly educated and trained about the potential for Aboriginal communities and families to provide more appropriate solutions to family healing.

(v) Requiring that all child-welfare decision makers consider the impact of the residential school experience on children and their caregivers.

Tosh has two things to say about the TRC's calls to action. First, these are not recommendations. A verb propels the phrase: *calls* demand movement. Tosh feels that language puts everything into motion. And that makes all the difference to the spirit of the document.

Second, many of the report's calls to action center on education.

And she reiterates: *Education is a space of transformation.*

▪ ▪ ▪

I do not feel, on this day in the archives, clear about my role. I go scrap to scrap. I try to listen. What I've elsewhere called a "robust research agenda" and now call, haltingly, "my day?" consists of no more and no less than: show up. Try to do it in a good way.

In the archives I read letters from 1912. The bishop of Yukon writes to someone in the south to ask for free chickens "so that the Indians can be self-supporting." The letter includes careful calculations about the freight of the chickens, recommends dimensions for their shipping coops, and explains plans to request free freight from the Canadian Express Company, at least as far as Vancouver. They want chickens because Chooutla staff are "anxious to make the training of the children as practical as possible."

Today, chickens.

Perhaps after a time I get lost in my inner clamoring. Maybe I blush. *Yes*, I probably agree with my thoughts, *the future will come. Canada will, in the future, organize a Truth and Reconciliation Commission to look at government-sanctioned social damage on par with apartheid.* Yes, that future—and others—will come. But in this letter the year is 1912, the subject is chickens, and the future is unknown.

I don't know exactly by what process we, the people, are to enter into relationship with the past. As I linger in the archives my intent becomes less driven. More basic. If the documents will speak, then what? I will listen? It's hard, bathed in the hubbub of the past's future, to really listen back in time.

Later staff letters detail flu symptoms (acute), fire damage (high), and garden productivity (low). A 1920 letter reports the death of a child to a father, informing a man somewhere, hundreds of miles away and over a hundred years ago, that he is now bereft of his son. Now.

I don't know how the chicken project panned out at Chooutla. Elsewhere I read of students sneaking off of school grounds to snare grouse, ptarmigan. In other words, they were hungry. And skilled.

I hold "copy B" of a March 20, 1920, letter typed on Chooutla Indian School letterhead from the school's principal, Reverend Dr. A. Grasett Smith. Eventually I'll notice the letter bears a title. In all caps at the top of the page are the words: "NIGHT LETTER." Sometimes urgency begets brevity. At this, my skin prickles.

"Influenza reported to Dr. Clark, sixteenth," reads the letter. "He wired you. My report mailed you. Two scholars ill, thirteenth, seventeen by sixteenth, all by seventeenth. . . . Three serious cases now, perhaps more later." The letter names staff, numbers days, and closes abruptly: "Everyone over-worked, need another helper."

Within the week, this same principal posts a letter to Chief Peter McGinty in Fort Selkirk, Yukon. From March 25, 1920:

> Dear Sir:–
>
> You have no doubt heard of the terrible epidemic of Influenza which has come over our school, as it has to so many other places.
>
> All our scholars were taken down with it, as well as four of the staff.

It was my sad duty to wire you that your son, Paul, had succumbed to the pneumonia which so often takes off those attacked with influenza.

I am sure it will be a sad blow to you and your wife, and I pray that the God of all comfort may be with you to comfort your hearts.

Everything possible was done for Paul. We have Miss Kipp, one of the Whitehorse nurses with us, and she was with Paul until the last.

We shall miss Paul sadly in the school, for he was a bright lad and a general favorite.

Enclosed you will find a few lines from Miss Bennett, Paul's matron, who also did all she could for him.

I am enclosing $2.15 the balance to Paul's account in the school box. We shall disinfect and send his things as soon as possible.

Believe me, yours in sympathy,
A. Grasett Smith
Principal.

■ ■ ■

Education may be a space of transformation but I also think about how transformation cuts more than one way. I think of Ovid; I think of his *Metamorphoses*. Transformation, whether suffered by a nymph, a woman, or a god, is often the result of rape or other attack. Sometimes, as when Daphne is transformed from water nymph into a laurel tree, transformation is the only escape from violence.

In other words, transformation is very often about survival, and survival comes at a cost.

Daphne loses her feet and grows roots; her pliable muscular body transforms into the stiff but living wood of a tree trunk. There's loss in the change, but it's a loss that leads to sovereignty. Daphne, thus transformed, escapes her aggressor. Alongside loss, then, lies both refuge and freedom.

■ ■ ■

I hear Linda's voice. *Chooutla's the oldest school in Yukon. It served the whole territory—except kids had to be status to go to Chooutla.* When she says the kids had to be "status" to go to Chooutla, she's referring to two legal categories: status Indians and non-status Indians. I must ask, *What?* Because Linda explains: *Yukon was formally segregated in schools. You have to know that.* Status Indians could not go to white schools. And non-status Indians could not go to status Indian schools.

A status Indian was formally registered under the Indian Act. It was a legal standing that granted education, certain tax exemptions, and health services. For decades, a status Indian woman was stripped of status if she married a white man. Their children would then be non-status. They may be integrated in their First Nations families and cultures, but the government called them non-status and denied them rights and services promised to their status relatives. Bureaucracy can, in fact, fracture families from the inside out. It can pit kin against one another.

I find an article online about the Yukon Association of Non-Status Indians, an association formed in 1972. "Losing status," I read, "resulted in lost rights, benefits and entitlements, including access to health care, housing assistance, justice supports, education funds and most important, loss of identity as a Yukon and Canadian Indigenous person."

Scattered conversations come to mind.

It's really only land claims that changed it, I hear, and I hear this over, and over, and over.

People say that land claims changed it—changed the specter of "status"—because Yukon First Nations insisted that their land agreements involve everyone, everyone, whether the federal government called them status or non-status. Yukon First Nations families were determined, in their land claims process, to be no less than precisely and simply that: family.

Of course I think of Alaska's land claims too, and of my hometown across the mountains on the coast on the Alaska side of the border. I think about the child-siloes dividing my classmates during my own early school years. I wonder what it would have been like to be an adult during that child time of mine, to observe the social fabric beyond the colorful block area and the school gym, beyond the music room and the swing set. A person standing on the Alaska-Yukon border in the 1980s could have looked both backward and forward in time. Alaska's land claims had begun the previous decade; Yukon's would begin in the next.

■ ■ ■

Some moments happen once.

Some moments repeat.

Again, it is my first day in the Yukon Archives. I wait at a long table for an archives technician to bring me Chooutla's public records from the stacks. The ceiling glows overhead, a tented shell between my long table and the sky. The archives technician arrives and unloads a series of trays, placing them before me. There are pamphlets, letters, a couple books. She stands opposite from me and leans over the boxes, lingering, curious to see what I pull out, curious to see what's there. We will talk and she will leave but in this version of the memory, the talking is central.

I open a folder. The pages inside are all hand drawn, hand decorated around some typewriter print. A whole sheet of signatures decorates page 2. *What is it*, she marvels, and I shake my head. I say that I don't know. It is true. I do not know what we are looking at.

We turn the pages over and around and pass them back and forth and eventually find these words: *Our First School Newspaper*. From the Chooutla Residential School in Carcross.

Ohhhhh, she says.

My grandma went there, she says.

And then my mom.

It stops with me, she says. *That's why I do my art. That's why I do my carving.* She mimes the curving scooping gesture of carving yellow cedar.

We are two women leaning across a table together, elbows splayed wide, heads bent close. I've come to the archives to learn, and to think, to do this at my own pace, and to do it without putting pressure on others to relive a painful past. I'm touched by the land's rocks and by its ice and I've come to the archives to do my due diligence with papers and pamphlets, to close my eyes and see how a document, like a rock, can break the silence.

My grandmother went there, she says, *and then my mom. It stops with me. That's why I do my art. That's why I do my carving.*

Her voice is steady.

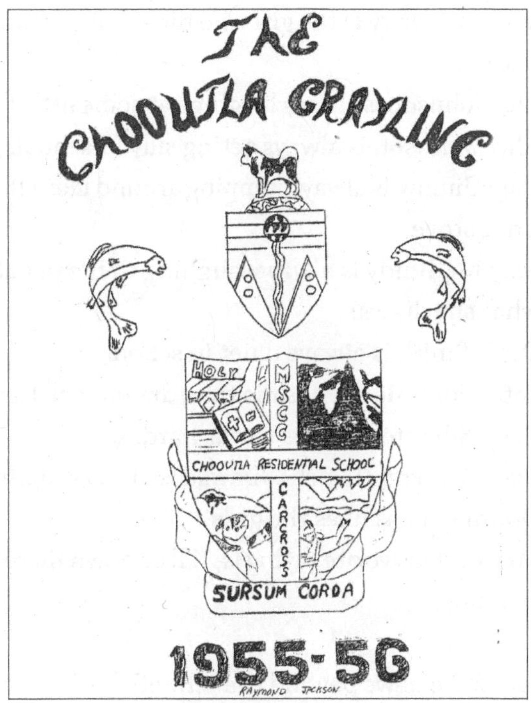

Image courtesy of Yukon Archives.

I came to hear the documents speak and they do. They sing out from the trays, they sing out from the first person standing next to me. That is how I meet the artist Lorraine Wolfe.

▪ ▪ ▪

A *Chooutla Grayling* school newspaper article by Sarah Smarch, grade 3, lists eleven stories about the children:

1. Sandra Sydney is the girl who hides rulers from the teacher.
2. Rita Johnson is always laughing at some little thing.
3. Alice Johnson is always acting silly in school.
4. Dave Jimmy is always jumping around like a flea on a hot stove.
5. May McGundy is always laughing to herself about what she draws.
6. Doris Smith is always quiet in school.
7. Peter Johnnie spends his time drawing pictures.
8. Clara Silverfox always works hard.
9. Blanche Lynn (Lynch) Jimmie is always smiling.
10. Donnie Burns likes the girls.
11. Mrs. Catt's favorite saying is, "I'll be down there with the ruler."

And what of the news beyond the school?

An October 15, 1959 news article, "Chooutla Roll Call Larger," discusses not only Chooutla in Carcross, Yukon, but also the school at Lower Post in northern British Columbia. At the time of its reporting, evidently 110 out of 180 Lower Post students are from Yukon, "relieving the burden" on Yukon's own schools like Chooutla.

It bears mentioning that Lower Post will, in later years, emerge as one of the most abusive residential schools in all of Canada. Evidence of the Catholic church's full complicity in physical and sexual abuse at Lower Post will be traced as far as Rome.

A May 21, 1964 newspaper photo caption reads: "Ten little nine little Indian boys . . ."[3] The caption is paired with a photo of shirtless kids, arms crossed, paper feathers taped to their heads. They are performing something for a group of visitors touring the school. Perhaps I shiver. Inside the world of the captioned photograph I am aware of the future, a future where child-me and all my classmates will also wear construction paper on our heads, paper similarly cut and colored to playact Nativeness.

About those paper headdresses. In *Appropriate: A Provocation*, Paisley Rekdal writes about artistic sampling and other cross-

3. About the photo caption, "Ten little nine little Indian boys. . . ." Nurseryryhmes.org provides all ten verses of the nursery rhyme, traces its initial publication to 1868, and notes the rhyme is "great fun" and "great for learning counting." If you don't already know it, the verses consist of small children who are at times "befuddled" and "fuddled" (depending on the verse), and who all eventually kick the bucket in various ways including a broken neck in one verse and shooting a kid in another. It is a song about systematic demise, abutting in the line "and then there were none." In short, the photo caption invokes two pretty solid stereotypes, one of Indigenous incompetence, and one of extinction. Nurseryrhymes.org helpfully suggests that if you are singing with girls, you can change the verses from "ten little Indian boys" to "ten little Indian girls," or, if you are singing with a mixed group of boys and girls, you may alternate between boy-verses and girl-verses.

cultural exchanges. In parsing the painful region where appreciation becomes appropriation, Rekdal warns against "stereotypes that link bodily and cultural difference with innate physical and mental characteristics." Beware, Rekdal argues, of markers that "*stand in metaphorically* for more profound, interior difference." Beware, in other words, of the paper feathers taped to boys' heads in the Sioux-derived look we recognize from Western cinema's oft-repeated cowboys versus Indians narrative. Beware of feathers that stand in metaphorically for the Indian-as-savage-or-at-least-as-buffoon, integral to the cowboy's winning plotline.

When child-me and all my classmates wear paper headdresses in the early 1990s, they are not styled like Hollywood feathers. We split the class in two; half wear an eagle design and half wear a raven design to mark the two moieties indigenous to our location. I wonder, though. I wonder. What was that paper headdress activity about? Why did we do it? Was it . . . respectful? I search my memory. I search.

I am interested in understanding my own life. I am interested in understanding my experiences. But when a fog shrouds the personal it's time to back off and come around again—at a slant. I'm saying: A wider, shared past is always there for the pondering. The uncertain personal is, after all, probably nested inside of it.

I page, then, toward the research file's next newspaper clipping. A 1968 article, "Yukon Experiment in Team Ministry," mourns the past and examines the future in which "a new concept of 'mission' is being created." The article is strange and troubled and for that reason, resonates. But inscrutably, it ends like this:

> The main challenge that any member of a team ministry will have to encounter is lack of response and concern. When faced with discouragement, the members of the Church in Carcross renew their valour by recalling the words of prophecy one of our number noticed inscribed on a washroom wall in Whitehorse: GOD IS NOT DEAD. HE'S HIDING IN CARCROSS.

Diffuse malaise in the file's news clippings won't give me much to grasp until it crystallizes in an October 21, 1981 headline that reads: "Mission Schools Produced Rootless Generation." Now I see the seeds of familiarity, though this language of "rootlessness" will yield to "displacement." In other words, this line of thought will evolve and it will become my recognizable present. "The school was run by well-meaning people," the article explains, "but people incapable of dealing with 300 children from a strange culture."

I sit in the archives paging through materials brought to me in trays and lingering on scraps that catch my eye. It's unscientific. Eventually it occurs to me that sifting scrap to scrap feels less like doing research—and more like showing up for a difficult relationship. I do not feel myself "researching" so much as attempting to stay present, to be in the moment, and to find traction, meaning connection, where it happens to arise.

■ ■ ■

If the best verb for this essay's unfolding is no longer "to research," then perhaps it is "to conjure." I sit in the archives, paging through trays, conjuring . . . silk strands, perhaps, something that resembles a spider web, both home and trapeze, gleaming paths strung corner to corner pulled tight so that we can all walk in sticky safety through open air, abyss all around. Abyss all around and yet averted.

■ ■ ■

Perhaps I ask Lorraine something about her grandmother and her mother, and perhaps I ask something about her carving, but of course these go hand in hand and now we are talking about art and the world's essential forms and crucially, the grain of the wood.

I love the high cheekbones, Lorraine says, pulling the skin of her own face. *And the straight mouth*. She holds her index and middle finger at attention, placing her two straight fingers across her own lips. She explains that she is a keeper of classical forms, the high classic rules and ratios.

She's working now on a moon mask. She'll bring it to the archives on her next work day. I can stop in and see it then.

I see Lorraine's hand scooping the air. I recall that Daphne became a tree. Sap-filled and rooted, body strong along the grain of the wood, the grain of sovereignty.

But carving seems like a reversal of Daphne's transformation. While Daphne escapes her aggressor by becoming wooden, carved wood reveals a face. Where Daphne loses her form for safety, Lorraine transforms yellow cedar into a story coded with the lines and curves of a formline moon.

One may go to the archives to find traces, marks from the past, texts with memories. One may go for the ghosts. One may go to the archives and end up involved with life living life, life flushed here and calloused there, malleable, simple, water-soaked life rushing along, in full swing, right now, here, wheeling along under the flat black mouth of the moon which is, in real life, somewhere just past this translucent ceiling.

It stops with me. Lorraine said. *That's why I carve.*

And then Lorraine returns to her desk. She is, of course, in the middle of her workday.

■ ■ ■

I read 1914 instructions from the deputy superintendent general of Indian Affairs suggesting "separate colonies" for ex-pupils.

What is an ex-pupil? A graduate?

Clearly, not.

Historian Kenneth Coates writes this of Chooutla: "The concerted effort to improve native hygiene and to inculcate different work habits of necessity called into disrepute the mannerisms and standards of the children's parents. . . . Ironically, though supposedly educationally prepared to re-enter native society, the students were taught through the residential school to abhor that environment, to look with disrespect if not disgust upon their families' customs."

Coates considers the words of a summer missionary at Carmacks. In 1934 that missionary noted students "are potential outcasts of their own people and are not quite up to the standards of the white intellect. In other words, they are 'betwixt and between'—a condition of pitiful helplessness."

Ultimately, Coates reads his way into the crevices of Chooutla's missionary perspective. He concludes that "most missionaries privately acknowledged that the residential school children could not be left entirely to their own devices," that missionaries recognized their students' "unenviable challenge ahead," and, importantly, that "the post-graduation experience of the Carcross Residential School graduates was difficult for the missionaries to accept."

Here, in the 1914 deputy superintendent general of Indian Affairs letter I'm looking at, the superintendent proposes that ex-pupils could inhabit separate colonies so they are "removed to some extent from older Indians." He writes not of graduation but of "discharge." "The Department requires that there should be careful preparation in this most important event in the life of a school pupil," he writes.

I suppose I see here the professionalism of an administrator handling a delicate situation. Earlier, I saw the elaborate attention given to chicken shipping. And I saw a third grader's inventory of her classmates' dispositions.

But I'm aware of Canada's Truth and Reconciliation Commission, its national effort at reckoning with the schools' human rights violations. I'm aware of today's headlines that repeatedly announce unmarked graves found at closed residential school sites. I'm aware of the assimilationist and genocidal policies driving US and Canadian residential schools. I may have gone to the archives in search of a more functional or tangible relationship with the past. But now that I'm here, it's the future that looms.

We talk about historic context. We say the past is a valuable way of understanding the present. It can tell us how things got to be the way they are. But what about the inverse? What about futuristic context? Is it actually the future that tells us what on earth happened in that dimly lit past that today simply soaks us to the bone?

I have to accept that my time in the archives has little to do with research. It's humbling but true. Others have done the research. And they will continue it. Instead, my time in the archives is existential, born from my sense that a shared future here, on the North's uneasy, melting ground, requires us to enter into right relations with divisive histories. Requires us to pitch in and help carry the difficult past.

▪ ▪ ▪

Next week I will return to the archives to see Lorraine's carving. She will have a clear plastic tote at her desk and she'll open it up, show me the moon mask she's working on. It will smell good. She'll put her index and middle finger together, hold them across her mouth again.

I love the straight lips. The classical forms, she says.

And she says this, too: *After Chooutla, my grandmother and my mother didn't know how to raise me up. They didn't know how to make me strong. But still, they made me strong. They couldn't make me strong. But they* did *make me strong. And I made my own children strong.*

They could not make her strong but still they made her strong. Yes. That is what she said.

Let's parse this. In the present tense, a grandmother and mother cannot make a girl strong—they don't know how to raise her up. In the past tense, they did it anyway. They made her strong.

Is history really about the past? I lose track sometimes of whether time moves backward or forward.

It stops with me, Lorraine said. *That's why I carve.*

Later, she will finish the moon mask. She will paint it white and black. Northwestel, the telephone company, will name her a Directory Art Winner, featuring a photograph of her carving "Tlingit Moon" on the cover of its 2020–21 phonebook.

It means that at the height of isolation in a global pandemic, if you want to talk to someone—anyone—in Yukon or northern British Columbia, the first thing you must do is find that form-line moon. Find the mask of yellow cedar transformed into the face of a story, yellow cedar scooped and sharpened and sanded and painted. Then turn the page. And look behind it.

GOVERNMENT DOCUMENTS: A LINEAGE OF BLADES

The artist makes sculptures out of government documents. She uses land use designation maps. Legal texts. And so on.

Her medium: papier mâché.

Her method: the tearing and pasting of paper. The tearing and pasting of documents.

She works to the sound of paper ripping, paces her thinking by the ooze of thick glue. She rips, reassembles; rips, reassembles. Papier mâché refuses clean lines. Yet the method performs the basic twinning gestures I can't get out of my head: destroying and connecting, dividing and binding.

In 2019 I sit in an audience's second row, pressed elbow to elbow against the person next to me and he to the person next to him, and so on. Our rows of too-close chairs create a temporary theater in the far end of a spacious art gallery. The artist is alone on the stage that our seating arrangement implies. She speaks. We listen. As planned.

Then she distributes copies of a text and directs the audience to read it aloud. We do. *Cede, release, and surrender*, we read. And while reading aloud joins us physically to the document, it also prompts a mental distance. We hear ourselves over and over—*cede, release, and surrender*—and grow perplexed. This is page 15 of the Umbrella Final Agreement, the document adopted in 1990 by the Yukon Territory to guide its First Nations land claims settlements.

Some weeks ago I skimmed all three hundred pages of this law. Like many laws, it is a ponderous read. But as I speak page 15 aloud, my skin prickles. This is, of course, the artist's object. And so it occurs to me that by the sound of our voices we've arrived at the edge of the knife, the thinned-to-translucence place of power in this document. The blade.

■ ■ ■

No Indian treaties were signed in Yukon. But in the bigger picture of North America, we live in a present called "the modern treaty era." A reprise of government-to-government negotiations centers on land, who it belongs to, and who belongs to it. Political scientists and culture bearers alike refer to this current chapter, the modern treaty era, as a time of formal severances.

It occurs to me that a severance, however abrupt it may be, is not a simple thing at all. Take severance at its most literal. The word invokes an instrument, carefully refined and made to cut. The word invokes a blade.

■ ■ ■

Physical blades tell a great deal of Yukon's archaeological history. Other traces of the past exist, of course, and still the story comes back to blades.

Archaeologists recognize the ancients by the blades they wielded, the blades they broke, the blades they left behind. Kinds of people; kinds of blades.

It starts with rock and bone. Then comes metal. These are the most essential materials with which to scrape, to sever, to open, to pry, to peel, to whittle, to carve, to cut.

Archaeologists may tell you they just pick up blades because that's all that's left. They may brandish spreadsheets or pledge allegiance to methodology sections. But catch one in twilight. Catch one half underground. An archaeologist knows that to understand people, you must read into their blades because a blade is a document that tells you who made it and how they lived. To know a people, you must read into the sharpest edges of the instruments by which they make their most essential cuts.

Imagine my surprise when I find out that is only one side of the coin. From Keavy Martin's book *Stories in a New Skin*, I learn that in hunting cultures, inherent in severance lies suturing.

To kill an animal—properly, Martin explains—a hunter severs that animal's life from its body. The animal dies. And this binds that animal's life back to the body of the hunter twice over: first in eating, because the animal's flesh becomes meat and nourishes the hunter, and second in clothing, because the animal's skin and fur supply essential shelter.

Which is perhaps why you can learn so much about a people by studying what they wear, how they cut materials from plants and animals and piece them back together into human forms. Of course humans, naked, are fragile. But clothed in the skins of others, humans find home everywhere on earth.

The blade is thus the first and most essential instrument by which to create both severance and kinship in one swipe.

Martin uses that metaphor in a book of literary criticism. But me, I am thinking about the law. And in the context of formal legal severances, I am very interested in Martin's certainty that connection—kinship, even—is what springs from severance itself.

■ ■ ■

In classical Chinese literature, we encounter Chuang Tzu's parable of the dexterous butcher. The butcher demonstrates that a knife with no thickness needs no sharpening. A great lord asks the butcher how this is possible. The butcher says he looks at oxen not with his eyes but with his spirit. He thus perceives neither flesh nor joints, but the spaces between. This line of sight permits him to strike the big hollows of an ox, guiding his knife through the openings, touching neither ligament nor tendon nor bone. The dexterous butcher is indeed quite dexterous. It is not clear what the great lord thinks of this.

▪ ▪ ▪

The lineage of blades in Yukon goes at the very least as far back as the microblade makers. Ten thousand years ago. Or fifteen thousand years ago. Or maybe more, or, maybe a people still more ancient lived here with another kind of blade entirely. Archaeologists are, of course, always digging. And the past is, of course, always changing.

In contrast, mine is a quiet and bookish search. I follow a local lineage of blades and it leads me to the microblade makers. I learn that we recognize them by their razor blades of stone: each microblade is a tiny, specially-shaped flake. It has two perfectly straight sharp edges, is perhaps an inch and a half in length, and only a quarter inch wide.

They live in another world, you know. Before things get to be the way they are now. For the microblade makers Yukon is an arid, subarctic savannah—a tiny-flowered and bunchgrassed place. Not a forested thing at all.

So it is that the microblade makers step quietly through grasses dotted with poppies and buttercups, cinquefoils and phlox. Tiny flurries of pink, white, blue, purple, and yellow shiver in the slanted summer light. Fescue and bluegrass and rye grass shush against peoples' legs when they stand tall, striding across the land.

So it is that the microblade hunters, when they stop to rest, lay down their blades now and again alongside flower petals, perhaps measuring the one by the other and the other by the one; perhaps gauging the perfection of a flower's curve against the precision of a stone point and perpetually finding, as the human mind will, uncanny connection between proximate things.

Many generations inhabit this aridity and watch its grassy openness grow speckled every summer with wildflowers.

And then it shifts.

The world grows warmer. The ice sheet shudders. Drop by drop, river by river, it melts. It recedes. So it is that with warmth comes moisture, the feathery sound of rain, the plunking of streams into creeks into rivers into lakes.

Bunchgrasses thin.

In their place, sphagnum moss thrives.

Generations of moss live and die and live and die. Generations of moss build up peat as grasslands recede, and this peat acts like a sponge, and bogs take shape along the low contours of the land.

And all the while, trees advance.

Willows.

White spruce.

Black spruce.

One day the steppe tundra is more like shrub tundra. Another day the shrub tundra is more like boreal forest.

And what of the microblade makers?

Well, they continue chipping their razor-thin flakes into perfect blades all the while. Grassland people become forest people.

Let us pause. Let us pause so that each razor may remind us that it was made and used by people who balanced upon the thin edge of a changing world, one that shifted ten thousand years ago from open, grassy tundra to dense boreal forest. Let us remember the microblade makers are the people who witness that change and who carry on, with a difference.

■ ■ ■

Kinds of people, kinds of blades.

A government document sometimes appears to be inert. It gets filed away; it sits in a binder. In this way, a government document assumes the appearance of a peaceful object.

But little is created from peace alone. Forces full of willpower and vision prompt a government document into existence. Shame and greed leap to the foreground, but sometimes these give way to responsibility and conviction and protection. Prompting a government document is always, to a degree, a force of subversion, and always, at the core, the force of desire.

■ ■ ■

A document, then, is a blade to peel back the sky.

It scrapes at the aurora, which falls curl by curl to the floor. It pries off each star with the tip of its knife; they fall and scatter toward the corners of the room.

Of any blade, remember this: used with precision, it will remain sharp enough to cut even the light.

■ ■ ■

Kinds of people; kinds of blades.

The Umbrella Final Agreement is Yukon's guide to settling Indigenous land claims. It was introduced to create fourteen sovereign First Nations governments, to delineate land ownership, to define land management powers, and to put government responsibilities and services into First Nations hands. The document is indeed a far-reaching umbrella under which falls the future, the past, and all the rest.

But Yukon's land claims do not start with the 1990 UFA. The seeds of Yukon's land claims are sown almost a generation earlier, when a group of First Nations leaders write a letter titled "Together Today for Our Children Tomorrow." They travel great distances and suffer great hardship to personally deliver this letter to the Yukon government.

The human experience is a story in itself. I do not know it. But I do know the document.

"Many of our people"—write the Yukon Indian people in 1973—"feel that our grievances are so great that there is no way we can be compensated for what has happened to us. This, we ask you to try to understand and to respect." In their words:

> About three hundred years ago the first Whiteman affected our way of life. We did not see these people but they changed our way of life. They were the Russians who traded with the Coastal Indians. These Indians then came over the mountains and traded with us.
>
> In 1973 . . . the Yukon Indian people are not a happy people. Both the Whiteman and the Indian are becoming more and more disgusted with each other. The Communications gap, the Social gap, the Economic gap—all these are widening. Both Indian and

> White are getting nervous because of the lack of understanding and tolerance among both groups.
>
> Being squeezed in by neighbors, White or Indian—separates us from the open land. We have a home for each season and cannot spend twelve months in one place.
>
> Many Whitemen say we do not care for our children. They point to Welfare, Truancy, and Juvenile Delinquency statistics to prove their point. Nothing could be further from the truth. The main concern of Indian parents today is what is happening to our children. We do not know because you are not telling us what you are doing to them. You take them to school, they go to your movies and dances, they watch your television and hang around your poolrooms. You told us they had to learn to live like Whitemen, so we did not interfere. You said our way of life was dead and that we had nothing to teach them. Please tell us what you are doing to our children, because they are breaking our hearts.

■ ■ ■

In how many ways does a child resemble a blade?

■ ■ ■

"Together Today for Our Children Tomorrow" doesn't really read as a government document. Fitting—it was penned not by a government, but by a people. Maybe "Together Today for Our Children Tomorrow" reads as some kind of sermon and maybe it reads as some kind of prophecy through which ferocity and tenderness pours, and pours, and pours.

The Umbrella Final Agreement, in contrast, is a technical, government document. It codifies the creation of Indigenous self-governments, sovereign ones. And it resolves land claims by determining who owns what parts of the land, dividing and assigning different degrees of power in questions of land management.

But technicality gives rise to paradox in the UFA's "cede, release, and surrender" clause—the one we read aloud in the art gallery. It says that in order to receive political control of traditional lands, a First Nation must first cede, release, and surrender those lands to Her Majesty the Queen of England.

Canada did not fight a revolutionary war. And so it bears mentioning that Canada's legal system maintains a working relationship with that monarchy across the sea.

This is to say that signatories—First Nations agreeing to the terms of the UFA in order to move forward through its processes to create a sovereign government and receive formal land rights—begin that multi-year process by *ceding, releasing, and surrendering* . . . everything. They sign it all away. This opens the door to formal negotiation, a process in which some of what's been ceded, released, and surrendered, will, under various provisions and rules and conditions, be formally returned.

The modern treaty era, remember, is a time of formal severances.

But if we take Keavy Martin's view of severance and suturing to heart, then maybe there is some sense in which this time of formal severances is by necessity also a time of formal suturings.

Perhaps this is a moment—like any other—which we may understand more clearly by noting, as archaeologists do, the things that cut. Because these may also be the things that connect. And so I take as object of study a lineage of blades, which becomes a lineage of government documents.

▪ ▪ ▪

Kinds of people; kinds of blades.

Who, then, are you and I?

I think of the deepest cuts of the present, legal ones, those that govern today's lives in the forested mountains of the Yukon, British Columbia, Alaska. I think of the deepest cuts of the present and the blades that draw them. And I begin to look for reciprocities binding that which our documents so crisply divide.

▪ ▪ ▪

Another blade comes to mind, the one surgeon and essayist Richard Selzer describes. Contemplating his scalpel's incisions into bodies laid bare upon the operating table, Selzer writes that "the blade draws like a slender fish. . . . It darts, followed by a fine red wake."

The blade *draws*, Selzer says. As if a knife were the instrument of an artist. An instrument always one step ahead of the artist's hand that wields it.

■ ■ ■

Take for example the Anglo-Russian Convention of 1825. The nineteenth century is a century of documents—but make no mistake. A document is not text alone; it is always already another kind of blade. A document is a blade to peel back the sky.

The Anglo-Russian Convention of 1825 attempts to define what has since become Southeast Alaska from what has since become the Canadian province of British Columbia and the Canadian territory of Yukon. It is the first Western document to cut this land. It is made to hold peace between competing fur traders, Russians and Brits. Having agreed on various lines across lands they did not really know, they slept easy. They knew already the boundaries would be paper thin yet strong enough to split even the wind itself.

Crucially, the convention exists between distant people who do not actually live here. No one who *does* live here has to contend with it. But the convention is a kind of origin story in itself because it sets forth principles that will direct the future of boundary-making in these borderlands.

One such principle of the 1825 Anglo-Russian Convention reads: "The said line shall ascend to the north along the channel called Portland Channel as far as the point of the continent where it strikes the 56th degree of north latitude."

Another: "The line of demarcation shall follow the summit of the mountains situated parallel to the coast as far as the point of intersection of the 141st degree of west longitude."

And of "the summit of the mountains," an admittedly ambiguous region: "The limit . . . shall be formed by a line parallel to the winding of the coast."

The line shall *ascend* (to the north). The line shall *strike* (the fifty-sixth degree). The line shall *follow* (the summit), and it shall *parallel* (the winding of the coast).

In fact, the line shall set out with a whole knapsack of verbs. Its journey will be long and arduous. Little line, seize the active voice and hold it close because you will ultimately have to reach 1,538 miles.

Imagine a sculpted lump of confidence stretched that far. A thing in the world, a thing upon a desk, a thing passed from one set of hands to another—a *real thing* made to span 1,538 miles—it must be pulled quite thin, wouldn't you say? Stretched to total translucence, I'd wager. Pinned and pulled and teased and spun thinner and finer and thinner and finer. Set down as surely as spider silk.

■ ■ ■

The 1867 British North America Act establishes Canada as a self-governing entity within the British Empire. The 1867 Treaty with Russia for the Purchase of Alaska transfers colonial claims to Alaska out of Russian hands and into American ones. The upshot is that in 1867, all at once, Canada became Canadian (no longer British). And Alaska became American (no longer Russian).

This is to say that the Anglo-Russian Convention of 1825—which established principles by which to demarcate the boundary between Russian-claimed territory and British-claimed territory—became the interpretive responsibility of neither Russia nor Great Britain but of the US and Canada.

Regarding the exact location of that boundary demarcating Southeast Alaska from British Columbia, unremarkably, American and Canadian ideas diverged. Both wanted the exact boundary to favor them—both wanted more land. Still, the disputes rang hollow and for thirty years didn't matter much at all.

Then came the Klondike Gold Rush of 1898–99. With thousands of southerners stampeding across Alaska and British Columbia into Yukon, questions of jurisdiction and lawlessness and responsibility grew urgent. That is when the exact location of the national boundary mattered very, very much.

■ ■ ■

From "Together Today for Our Children Tomorrow":

> This is a Settlement for tomorrow not for today. We have tried to tell you some of the reasons why we will not be able to solve our problems immediately.
>
> . . . You cannot talk to us about the "bright new tomorrow," when so many of our people are cold, hungry, and unemployed. A "bright new tomorrow" is what we feel we can build when we get a fair and just Settlement. Such a Settlement must be made between people of peace. There must be a "will-to-peace" by all the people concerned. We feel we have shown this "will-to-peace" for the last hundred years. If you feel the same, it should be easy

> for us to agree on a Settlement that will be considered "fair and just" to all. If we are successful, then the date of our agreement will be a day for all to celebrate—in the years to come. Public holidays now have little meaning to the Indian. August 17—Discovery Day (the Yukon's Territorial Holiday) means to the Whiteman the day the gold rush started. It means to the Indian the day his way of life began to disappear.

■ ■ ■

During the lawless heyday of the 1898–99 Gold Rush, a joint commission failed to resolve the Canada-US border dispute.

In 1903 they tried again. The Hay-Herbert Treaty called for a six-member tribunal made up of three Americans, two Canadians, and one British member to make a decision. They did. At present, the 1903 outcome of the Alaska Boundary Tribunal is what's down on all the maps.

In fact, it is difficult to find a map of these northern forested mountains that omits the hard black lines delineating US state from Canadian province, US state from Canadian territory, Canadian province from Canadian territory.

■ ■ ■

The Alaska-Yukon border continues northward from the odd arrangement separating Southeast Alaska's coastal rainforest from British Columbia's inland forests. It runs due north from Mount Saint Elias along the 141st meridian of longitude to the Arctic coast, dividing people, migration routes, and weather systems the whole way. Of course the line is razor-thin; more a concept than a physical entity. For example, I meet a man whose grandfather's house was mathematically divided by the line—he'd sleep in Yukon and make morning coffee in Alaska, or something to that effect.

I meet him because I attend a long-form Q and A session in which he is one of two leaders from non-signing nations—nations that so far have not signed on to the UFA. There is a full audience, there are cameras, there are microphones, and there are pitchers of water and glasses and armchairs set up before an arranged backdrop.

I listen to the interview, the conversation. But that is the smaller part. The larger part is that I see, perhaps for the first time, government physically imprinted on two people. The speakers, leaders of non-signing nations, are exhausted. It is visible.

Two things occur to me. First, I realize the men in these armchairs speaking in 2019 devoted much of their lives to the slowness and repetitiveness of functional democracy. And because there is no end to negotiations in sight, they will carry on.

Second, I realize there is no rest for the weary because the legacy of their people—past, present, and future—hangs in the balance. They think of their people on a larger scale than the overculture's systems and language can account for.

Genuinely invested in the well-being of non-signing nations, audience members present as allies hatch many versions of the same question. *Tell us again why not signing is still the best thing to do right now*, people say. As if "right now" lay separate from the grandbabies who inherit each of our acts as their history.

The speakers, leaders of non-signing nations, do not carry such a sense of "right now." They think, act, and pause on a multi-generational scale. And they say so over, and over, and over before the cameras, the microphones, the pitchers of clear water, and the arranged backdrop. The leaders bring a quietude to the dissonance, and a certainty, and a poise.

Here we are. All of us. In the conversation. A conversation that has yet to develop a shared language. A conversation in which even the word *now* contains so much slippage that a dizziness takes hold.

Though it was penned nearly fifty years ago, "Together Today for Our Children Tomorrow" explains exactly this slippage quite clearly. The document includes an inventory of "gaps," such as the social gap, the economic gap, and so on. The sixth item is the communications gap:

> COMMUNICATIONS
>
> We want to mention this problem separately because of our feelings about what is happening to us today.
>
> We listen to Whitemen from the time we get up till we go to bed. Most of this is one-way communication. It is Whitemen talk—Indian listen—we listen to radio, teachers, politicians, clerks in stores, television, music, salesmen, etc. They are all salesmen, trying to sell the Whiteman's way. We don't have a chance to think, let alone a chance to answer.
>
> We are being brainwashed that White is right and Indian is wrong. This must be changed. There must be two-way

> communication between us. We cannot talk to you as equals when you are living in your big house and we don't even have a job.
>
> With a just Settlement of our claims we feel we can participate as equals, and then we will be able to live together as neighbors. We feel we can teach the Whiteman much, just as we have done in the past.

■ ■ ■

A timeline.

Canada's federal government signs the 1990 Umbrella Final Agreement. The government of Yukon signs. The Council of Yukon First Nations signs. Finally, a formal framework. Now it is up to each of the fourteen individual First Nations to negotiate their own specific agreements—and sign them.

In 1992 four First Nations sign self-government agreements. They are the First Nation of Nacho Nyäk Dun, Champagne and Aishihik First Nations, Vuntut Gwitchin First Nation, and Teslin Tlingit Council.

In 1998 three more First Nations reach agreements and become self-governing: Little Salmon-Carmacks First Nation, Selkirk First Nation, and the Tr'ondek H'wechin First Nation.

In 2002 another nation finalizes its agreements—the Ta'an Kwäch'än Council signs.

And another in 2003. The Kluane First Nation signs its self-governing agreements.

In 2005 two more First Nations seal the deal. The Kwanlin Dün First Nation and the Carcross/Tagish First Nation sign their respective agreements.

At present eleven First Nations have signed. They have formally established themselves as self-governing entities.

Three have not signed on to the UFA and remain in negotiations. They are the White River First Nation, the Liard First Nation, and the Ross River Dena Council.

■ ■ ■

"Many of our people"—write the Yukon Indian people in "Together Today for Our Children Tomorrow" (1973)—"feel that our grievances are so great that there is no way we can be compensated for what has happened to us. This, we ask you to try to understand and to respect."

■ ■ ■

Let us return to the far corner of a spacious art gallery. The forty-eight chairs in curving rows. The artist, also a political scientist, whose tears run as she speaks. Each chair sat in, sat upon, and stacks of additional chairs wheeled in on dollies at various points in the talk.

We've read the "cede, release, and surrender" clause of the UFA. The technical document is lodged, if you will, in our throats. And now the artist tells her story.

Of course it is not my story. It is hers. I have heard her tell it, several times, in public, to a gathered audience. And I think about it.

I remember the story like this:

The artist gave birth. Then she wanted to give her placenta back to the land. But her aunties did not know the ceremony; they did not know the way for her to give her placenta back to the land. Residential school severances. The knowledge was lost.

But they knew someone who knew someone, and so on. And the artist asked again, and again, and again, and one day, she found a ceremony through which her people gave their placentas back to the land.

So she invited her family. They went out on the land. She taught them all the parts of the ceremony. "Did we do that?" they asked one another, wondering, and the artist was quiet and pleased that she could teach them. "Yes," she could answer. "Yes, this is the way we gave our placentas back to the land." Together that is what they did, they gave her placenta back to the land, tied her body and her son's body to a special place.

This is what I imagine: The widening circles of the artist's family joined the ceremony and learned it and practiced it, and the ancient-new knowledge rose in one clean wave over the residential schools' severance. I imagine the ceremony washed over the wound in one clean rinse. Maybe even joined its edges. Readied it for suturing. That is what I imagined the first time I heard the story, that is what I imagined the second time I heard the story, and that is what I imagine still.

Though of course that is not the end of the story.

Later, the artist would look at a map.

A map drawn from a government document.

She would learn from this map that the land to which she gave her placenta was classified as "category two."

"Category two land is legally designated for mineral development," says the artist to the audience. Not protected. Rather, predesignated for extraction.

One artist. Also a political scientist. A professor, an educator. A mother. A seeker of the old ways, and so also a healer. She speaks publicly about her placenta, searching for a ceremony, finding it, giving her placenta back to the land, sharing the ceremony with her whole family, galvanizing her nation. But this is how she ends the story every time I have heard her tell it. The artist tied her body to the land—and tied her son's body to the land—in a place marked on maps for the mining industry.

■ ■ ■

From the text of "Together Today for Our Children Tomorrow":

> What is different between Canada's treaties (signed in the prairies) and the Yukon:
>
> This time it is different, because the Government of Canada has asked us to say what our position is.
>
> First, remember, there were never any wars between Indian and White in the Yukon.
>
> Second, remember, there were no treaties signed in the Yukon.
>
> Third, remember, the first Indian Act was designed to protect the Indian from the Whiteman. This concept was never applied in the Yukon.
>
> These three things are important, because they combine to make the YUKON claim different from other Settlements.

The objective of the Yukon Indian people is to obtain a Settlement in place of a treaty that will help us and our children learn to live in a changing world.

We want to take part in the development of the Yukon and Canada, not stop it. But we can only participate as Indians. We will not sell our heritage for a quick buck or a temporary job.

We must have, both the right to be different, and the right to be accepted as fellow-citizens and as fellow-humans. Most of the time, Whitemen have insisted that we become instant Whitemen. This was never possible.

▪ ▪ ▪

Recall this of Chuang Tzu's dexterous butcher: His knife has no thickness. He tells his lord he works slowly, inserting this blade with no thickness into the spaces between. The dexterous butcher points out that in the spaces between, there is plenty of room.

▪ ▪ ▪

Kind of people; kinds of blades.

Today, the modern treaty era. A time of formal severances.

A couple centuries ago, the Bennett Lake culture.

The Bennett Lake culture is composed of those who arrange their stone, bone, and copper points alongside scissors and kettles of brass. Alongside axes and knives and saw blades of steel and iron. They receive these tools through trade with their coastal neighbors who pass them on after having, in turn, received these in trade with Russian fur traders. Cutting, in this time, ties people to profoundly distant lands. Cutting, in this time, invokes a wide and widening circle of exchange and negotiation, friendship, influence, power, and desire.

And before the Bennett Lake culture, the Aishihik culture.

The Aishihik culture are the *small* notched-point makers. Their blades are made not for spears but for arrows. They also make small stone points with narrow stems, blades like leaves. And they make finely hammered bars of copper, thin as bookmarks, pointed at each end to catch in the throat of the fish that darts to swallow it. As if a fish, like life, were something we could stop midsentence and then return to, picking up where we left off.

Before the Aishihik culture were the notched-point hunters. They use throwing boards, atlatls, to hurl their spears with a new kind of stone point—one with a notch on each side of the base. The human world turns over when the notched-point hunters emerge. "In fact," writes ethnographer Catharine McClellan, "there are so many changes in the stone artifacts of the southern Yukon at this period, and the changes are so great, that it seems like an entirely new people had arrived in the country." Stone chopping tools and sinkers for fish nets abound among them, as do new forms for animal-skin scrapers.

And before the great human turn to the notched-point hunters? The microblade makers.

You remember them.

The microblade makers and their tiny stone flakes. Razors really. How they hunted in the subarctic grasslands adjacent to a vast ice sheet. How they balanced on the thin edge of a changing world, one that shifted from open, grassy tundra to dense boreal forest. People who lived by the cuts of knives so small, it was the world that simply shifted around them.

Perhaps that is something we have in common across the millennia. Some of those who lived here in the many shades of the deep past knew ecologic transformation. Knew it intimately. They received it, responded. Carried on.

And those who live here now know today's ecologic transformations. Know them intimately, even as we make our quiet preparations for uncertain futures. Uncertain futures that, strangely, may loop back toward the dry, open grasslands, which the earliest microblade makers knew so well.

Indeed some climate scientists suggest that today's boreal forests—the ones presently warming and drying at an extraordinary speed—may soon recede. The trees may . . . walk back. It's an open conversation. Climate scientists and forest ecologists and experts in general do not necessarily agree with each other. Yet there it is, an idea on the table. It seems entirely possible that today's increasing warmth and aridity harkens a return of the grasslands.

On a July afternoon in 2021, I am out on the land with a group of artists and scientists. We stand together, rubber-booted feet sunk into a boreal forest bog, looking up at a silty south-facing slope. It rises steeply above us, perhaps an old river bluff. The slope is fringed at the top with forest, unmistakable black spruce scraggle running rich and dark against the day's dry sky. Chill bog water pools around our boots where we sink a bit in the bog's orange-red carpet of sphagnum mosses and Labrador tea. For a time, we do not budge. We've paused in the bog to ponder the silty slope. It is so silty. A few wild roses grow in its sands. We watch their pink blooms dipping and hiccoughing in the wind. Sagebrushes and grasses grow too, in bunches scattered here and there. Otherwise, vegetation is sparse. The slope's bare patches of pale, silty dirt are as wind-blown as the rose blossoms.

As your own feet sink in the sphagnum bog, crane your neck. Look carefully at the dry, silty slope, wherever you may find it. Memorize the sagebrush's dusty green, the rustling bunchgrasses, the dotting pinks of wild roses, the near-seashell glow of pale, bare dirt. And imagine this patch of earth writ large. Can you see it? The way forward? Maybe it's somewhere like this, somewhere on the land, written into a south-facing slope perhaps, one made of pale sediments as soft and gritty as a grandmother.

The land has always been peopled. The people have always used knives. And the knives, one step ahead of the hands holding them, have always drawn across the field of skin into what the people must enter.

PART THREE

The Trails Are Always There

UNDER THE BRIDGE AT JOHNSON'S CROSSING

1.

Two things fill the sky: steel beams and swallows.

Erected in wartime to hold a highway, steel rises from the river bottom into a geometry of struts, stringers, and diagonals running clifftop to clifftop a hundred feet up. Legions of songbirds scissor the air, swooping and diving from the truss.

In the river's theater of erosion and deposition, nothing has ever been so solid as steel beams. In the forest's pulse of growth and decay, nothing has ever been so permanent.

Solidity and permanence. They pull a sorrow high into the air where swallows scissor and arc, scissor and arc.

But reader, perceive the nests. Mud huts pock every beam, every nut and bolt, the anchored cables, the seams joining steel to concrete. Does each tiny shelter rely on industry—or vice versa? Does the structure rely on mounds of earth and grass, on the nestlings within, on each blade-winged parent's continual return? Likely enough, yes. Likely enough, the bridge depends entirely on so many swallows' arcing lines of flight. It is their movement in the sky that sketches steel into existence over the river. It is their movement in the sky that holds the bridge's neat lines between clifftops.

II.

The steel bridge depends entirely on the swallows. Their mud nests connect the beams. Their sound thickens the air, supporting its reach from wartime to present.

I watch from the river's edge one hundred feet below. The bridge may depend on swallows but it seems unmoved by the pulse of the boreal forest. Fearfully solid. Permanent, even—like every mistake I have ever made. I see I am beginning to wish this bridge was as temporary as a swallow's line of flight.

Perhaps it can be. Perhaps the industrial structure is momentary. If there is hope against our mistakes, surely it lies in transience. Inherent disappearance.

This must be why I want to live in a world where it is the sound of swallows and their sound alone that supports the impossible weight of steel in the air. This must be why I seek the simple guarantee of loss.

That is when a loon cries out once. A loon cries out over still water under a sky of swallows busy upholding a bridge so history can find safe passage through the air. A loon cries out and the chill hits my core. That chill: that is this life's one permanence.

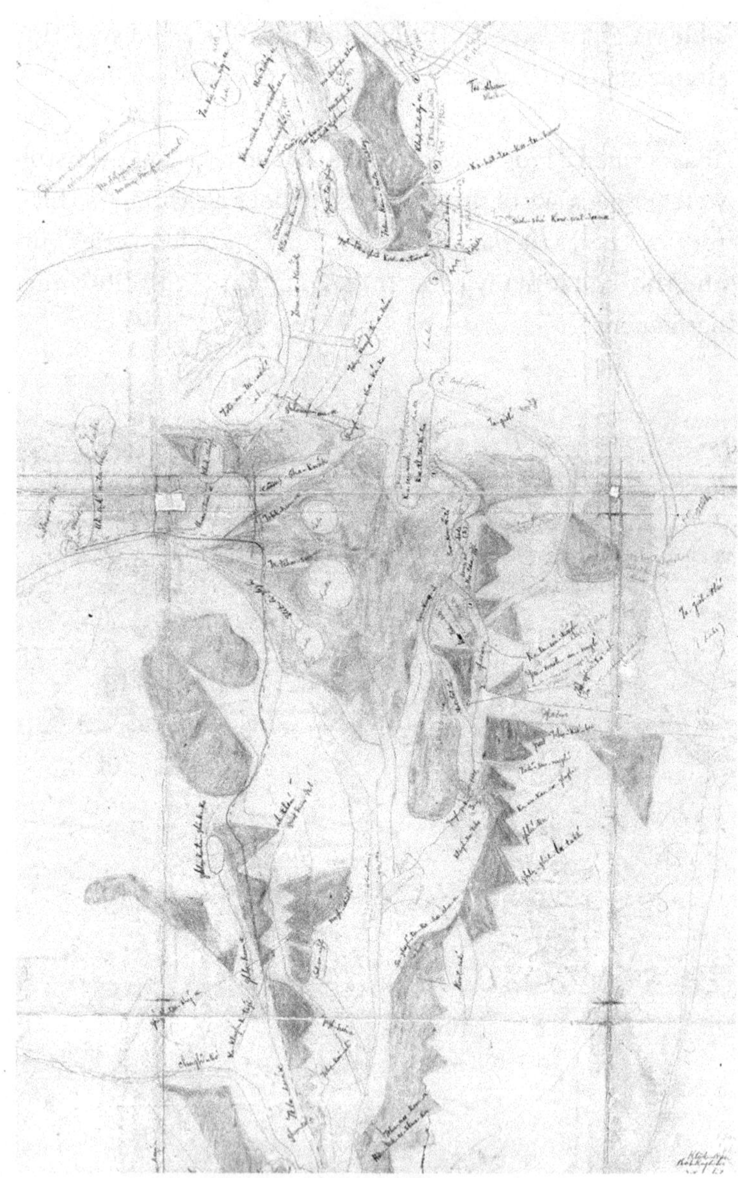

Image of Kohklux map (1869) courtesy of The Bancroft Library.

THE KOHKLUX MAP

I think of the map in many ways, but the most outstanding is how we bring our children up. Our Elders said: where your child and your grandchild will walk, pay attention to it so that child or grandchild will not have a hard time when they come to that place.

—Joe Hotch, Tlingit Elder, 1994

I. THE THREE

Deep in the Chilkat Valley three coastal people bend over the blank reverse of a coastal chart, discussing, drawing, shading, remembering. They are Chilkat Headman Kaalaxch' (Kohklux) and his esteemed wives, Tu_eek and Kaatchxich. It is August 1869. With the first pencil they have ever used, the trio spreads memory, spreads their ancestors' voices, spreads the land itself—from one end of the paper to the other.

To the south, the Takhinsha Mountains and Chilkat Range rise from sea to sky. Downriver lies Lynn Canal, a tempestuous but rich Pacific fjord. Upvalley, the trio pulls a pencil across the page and alongside them flow the frigid, milky waters of the Chilkat River. Hooligans, or candlefish, seasonally swell its current. To the north, the sheer rock faces and year-round snowfields of the Takshanuk Mountains stand hard against the sky.

Beyond those peaks the sky is solid and the universe, according to some, expands. Beyond those peaks the forest is not coastal rainforest—it is inland, boreal. Beyond those peaks that boreal forest is home to people who speak the many inland languages, sing the many inland songs.

For three days, three coastal mapmakers work. For three days they discuss among themselves, checking and double-checking each memory, checking and double-checking the timbre of their ancestors' voices, checking and double-checking the contours of generations to come. That is how I imagine it. Because I am trying to think: What does it take to draw those several hundreds of miles? To draw every forested turn of the land along the way? To draw the pooling lake waters and sinuous shorelines? To draw every ridgeline against every sky? Even the surface of things don't give themselves away to just anyone. Much less the shapes and the shadows.

11. PLUS ONE

The land they draw stretches all the way from Klukwan on the rocky shores of Southeast Alaska to Fort Selkirk on the sandy banks of the Yukon and Pelly Rivers. Headman Kaalaxch', Tu_eek, and Kaatchxich draw each day of the monthlong journey past those peaks, a journey from the shores of the frigid, milky waters of the Chilkat River on the rainforested coast all the way into the boreal-forested lands of people living far, far inland. They draw the journey from memory. With the first pencil they have ever used, they invent an entire visual shorthand for what their language already contains, has always contained.

Because their guest, George Davidson, doesn't speak Łingit. And he doesn't come from people who practice the art of remembering everything they hear. George Davidson speaks English, and he comes from people who trace their most sacred knowledge onto sheets of paper, which they bind into books, which they place in libraries.

One day I, too, will come from a long line of people who write things down. And I, too, will stand now and again on the banks of the frigid, milky waters of the Chilkat River. So I think back. I wonder about people and places, past and present. Present places full of past people. I think of standing where others stood before. I wonder what from their mingling passes into us.

But for now, there is no I. For now, it is 1869, and George Davidson watches.

He's given Headman Kaalaxch' and his wives, Tu_eek and Kaatchxich, the biggest sheet of paper he can procure, a coastal chart. The trio draws for three days on its reverse side. Across the broad page, they pencil everything from distinctive mountain profiles, to riverways and lakes, to meeting places with inland peoples. Kaalaxch', Tu_eek, and Kaatchxich know the land's features, their names in all the languages spoken across the route, and the way to find safe passage over the 2,500-foot-high mountain pass.

That is not all. They also own the trail as clan property. It belongs to them. And although pencil and paper are new tools for these three, the precision and accuracy of their hand-drawn map will stun local experts, GIS mappers, and geographers well over a century later.

But that is the future. For now, George Davidson watches, and then, he listens attentively to his hosts. He tries to learn place names along the route. He tries to learn instructions. Ultimately, he will transcribe over a hundred names and notes onto the map in multiple Indigenous languages, including Łingit, Tagish, Southern Tutchone, and Northern Tutchone. George Davidson bends his back as scribe.

It could not have been easy. In Łingit alone, there are at least eight distinct sounds for what the Anglo ear hears over and over again simply as a hard *k* sound. On top of that, there are another eight glottals, which a sensitive Anglo ear might register more like *ch*, or might simply hear as another round of repetitive *k* sounds. That makes as many as sixteen distinct Łingit sounds that an Anglo ear cannot distinguish. George Davidson, of course, has an Anglo ear. Still he listens; still he strains to hear. Probably for hours. Painstakingly he transcribes names and notes.

Some of his notes, speakers and linguists can decipher today. Some, they cannot.

Davidson and his party are here to observe a solar eclipse calculated to reach totality at Klukwan. That is, Davidson and his party want to look straight at the sun, take its mark and measure, learn something about our place in the universe, the place from which our strange small shared world does its spinning. For this occasion Kaalaxch' guided Davidson and his party from Sheet'-ká X'áat'l, Sitka, on the outer coast of Baranof Island, up Lynn Canal into Kaalaxch's homeland, to Klukwan, at the foot of North America's highest coastal mountains.

What lies between leaders like these? What is it that quietly joins these ambitious and powerful people, absent any shared language? Trust, perhaps. Maybe even recognition.

III. DEEP TIME, LONG AGO

Once, I sat among children and parents in a Whitehorse, Yukon hotel lobby. We gathered there for an art opening, and at the appointed time, placed the hotel's chairs into an oblong ring for storytelling.

Inland Tlingit Elder Shirley Adamson sat near a table of paintings. Children took turns picking first one painting, then another. With each choice, Shirley propped the painting on her knee and told us the story painted onto canvas.

Because I grew up close by—across the mountains on the coast in Juneau, about halfway between Klukwan and Sitka—I grew up with similar stories. I know, for example, that a raven brought light to the world, played the tricks, and so on. Still does. And I know that coastal people call him a raven while inland people call him a crow.

But of the land itself, all I knew was the faraway story of Turtle Island, knowledge held by North America's East Coast Algonquian people. I only knew about the muskrat who dove, returned with a ball of mud. I only knew about the turtle's back, the mud placed upon it, the resulting creation of Turtle Island.

The northernmost turtles I have seen sat in a row, on a log, in a pond near Cranbrook, British Columbia. By car, the turtles were twenty-seven hours south of Whitehorse. As the crow flies, they were over a thousand miles away. How, I wondered, could such far-off turtles hold up our spiny northern borderlands?

But in that hotel lobby with Shirley and a bright turquoise painting propped on one knee, I learned something essential: that the world was once all water and now there is land and that the land—like the light—was not made a thousand miles away in turtle habitat. It was made right here.

Shirley tells the story twice. A coastal telling and an inland telling. In both cases, the world is all water. In both cases, the trickster grows weary flying all day and all night with nothing to land on. Among coastal people, a raven tricks a sea otter. She brings him bottom-sand from the bottom of the sea; he throws it out on the water, dances his medicine, and makes land. It's been here ever since. Among inland people, it's not a raven but a crow, and he tricks not a sea otter but a seagull. Then the same things happen. The seagull brings him bottom-sand from the bottom of the sea, the crow throws it out on the water, dances his medicine, and makes land. It's been here ever since. Maybe you're standing on it now.

The center of the universe, then? It's been with us all along. Right underfoot. Organized as such:

Coastal	**Inland**
Biomes flanking the coastal side of the mountains: rainforests, muskegs, beaches.	Inland biomes, on the opposite slopes of those same mountains: boreal forests, marshes, clay cliffs.
Coastal weather: wet. Summers are not too hot and often a feather rain falls. Winters are not too cold and snow piles up high, high.	Inland weather: dry. Summers bake. Winters crack with cold.
Coastal abundance: a thing of the sea. Fish oils. The depths of a dark ocean infuses salmon, those flashing tides that return every summer to course up creeks, the once-annual throb of a heartbeat.	Inland abundance: a result of powerful temperatures. Winter means mammals, inland, grow incredible furs. The depths of a dark winter reverberate in the burrowing, galloping, densely furred forest animals.

Indigenous peoples in Yukon and Alaska have always traded their abundances. Coastal Tlingit people crossed the mountains into southwest Yukon carrying heavy packs loaded with cedar, shells, and especially hooligan oil. In fact, the oil-rich hooligans were so important that this coastal-inland route was dubbed "the Grease Trail." Southern and Northern Tutchone people met their Tlingit trading partners at well-known sites to exchange the inland biome's superior-quality furs, hides, copper, ocher, gopher robes, and skin clothing for the Tlingit's coastal resources. For the dark depths of the sea rich with oil, the dark depths of winter in thick furs and perfect pelts. They covered great distances to exchange goods, weaving thick ropes of interdependence over mountains that rise much higher than any forests can grow.

The over four-hundred-mile route that Kaalaxch', Tu_eek, and Kaatchxich mapped from Klukwan to the confluence of the Yukon and Pelly Rivers at Fort Selkirk represents, one way, a one-month journey.

But always remember that before all those long walks, the world was water and no one walked anywhere. They swam. Or they flew. It's only recently that the universe expanded into the land we walk on.

What, in the end, have we inherited in this? Continual transformation, for one. And a capacity for continuities to coexist with transformation, perhaps.

To conduct the trading, for example, each side designated leaders. There were protocols, expectations met and reenacted again and again across generations. Often, women had the final say in exchanges. After business was done, people celebrated with feasting and songs, dances, stories, regalia, and gifts. Marriages between Tlingit and Southern and Northern Tutchone people created cross-mountain, cross-language familial closeness. Strengthened business ties. Softened the borders between groups. Averted conflict. Eased the necessity of travel across others' lands. Positioned traders as kin, as relatives.

It occurs to me again, somewhere here lies trust. Trust of the truest sort. Not necessarily devoid of doubt—of latent skepticisms and jealousies, of greedy or unfair transactions, of grudges and resentments, no one can say. Certainly I can't. But somewhere here, *right here*, between travelers and hosts, across many languages, countless generations, and even wars, lies trust—rekindled, over, and over, and over. Recognition.

IV. A TIMELINE

Inside many generations of patterned exchange lies the Kohklux Map, its particular moment, its internal thresholds and turning points. I try to resee the story of the world, now on the maps' scale.

1869

At Sheet'-ká X'áat'l (Sitka) on the outer coast of an island we now call Baranof, Headman Kaalaxch' sketches a map on a sheet of notebook paper. But the page is far too small; he cannot put his mind to paper on that scale. Later, he escorts George Davidson up Lynn Canal into the Chilkat Valley—Kaalaxch's own homeland—where the party wishes to observe a solar eclipse. The group makes camp not too far from Klukwan. In the days prior to the eclipse, Kaalaxch' and his two wives, Tu_eek and Kaatchxich, draw the mountainous journey on the blank, reverse side of a large coastal chart. It takes them three days to draw it. The legacy: two maps—a smaller one frustrated by scale, penciled by Kaalaxch' alone, and a larger one, penciled by an expert trio over the course of three full days, *the* Kohklux Map.

They are the earliest known maps of southern Yukon.

They are also the first known maps committed to paper by Indigenous peoples in this region of the world. Which is to say, in this region of the universe.

And what of the 1869 solar eclipse? Well, we know at least this: It comes, and then it goes.

1901

Over thirty years after all this, George Davidson publishes an article about his experience on the banks of the frigid milky waters of the Chilkat River. He writes:

> In 1869 we made the trip up the Chilkaht to observe the total solar eclipse of August 7. At Sitka, through the kind offices of the military commander, General Jefferson C. Davis, we were brought face to face with Kohklux, the famous chief of the Chilkahts. . . .
>
> We selected the village of Klu-kwan', in 59 deg. 25 min., for the observations and, fortunately, we were enabled to use our Chinook jargon with the two wives of Kohklux; and in our interviews we learned that he had projected and carried out the destruction of the Hudson's Bay Company's station at Fort Selkirk on the 21st of August, 1852, because they had dared to interfere with his traffic with the Tahk-heesh and other interior Indians. This fact was unknown to the Canadians until we communicated it to Land Commissioner Ogilivie, in 1897.

> At his own suggestion Kohklux proposed to draw upon paper his route to and from Fort Selkirk. The second attempt was upon a large sheet, 43×27 inches. . . . It began at Point Seduction, in Lynn Canal, with islands, streams, and lakes; and with mountains in profile.

Davidson's article goes on to describe his party's journey with Kohklux from Klukwan "to the Tat-sae-heen'-a, below Fort Selkirk," naming every river, lake, and mountain that he can deduce, triangulating between his Tlingit guides' teaching and the government maps he carries.

Davidson's story dissipates there, recedes. I suppose there comes a time when one day he is alive and the next, dead. After, there remain boxes of what we call "his collected papers." Nothing much happens with them for about three generations.

1985

Yukon territorial archivist Linda Johnson finds—among George Davidson's uninventoried papers, housed in Berkeley, California's Bancroft Library—the Kohklux Map. The map itself has not been accounted for in perhaps a century. Bancroft Library has no idea that it holds such a map in its archives.

1987

The Bancroft Library agrees to send both Kohklux maps, the small and the large, to Yukon—on loan—for northern people to celebrate and study their heritages, their histories, their languages, and the magnitude of the cross-cultural moment those maps represent. A gathering, a celebration, a conference is planned, held, and remembered. Then the organizers return the maps to Bancroft Library who, in turn, returns the maps to a shelf in the archives.

But for this 1987 sojourn to Whitehorse, Yukon for a conference, the maps live in storage, climate controlled.

What of time? It passes, I suppose.

2018

I am on my own looking at art in Whitehorse, Yukon, and beginning in some slant way to write this book. I borrow a binder from a neighbor who previously took a class, flip through the course materials, read a short article about the Kohklux Map, pull a printed copy of the map from a sleeve of the binder, unfold it across my whole table, and become entangled. The shades and shadows. The eyeball-bending detail. The handwriting. Who can say. I tape the copy of the map to my wall. I begin living alongside it. And I start making phone calls. That is how I meet former Yukon territorial archivist Linda Johnson. *We're planning another conference*, she says. The year 2019 will be the 150th anniversary of the maps' making.

2019

For the better part of a year I observe (and attempt to support) conference planning. As a new volunteer for the Yukon Historical and Museums Association, I join local academics and history buffs alongside Canada Parks professionals, Yukon First Nations, and Alaska Native groups. We plan a 150th anniversary gathering. Like the one in the eighties—but more elaborate. It will be a cornucopia of linguistic research, historical pondering, cultural celebration, political leveraging, and everywhere will be conversation, conversation, conversation. My task: gather presentation proposals and cluster them into panels combining community knowledge with scholarly research. Pair local with visitor; arrange proximities and alignments. I am to set up conversations that will cross borders, cross fields, cross cultural expectations. I create spreadsheets and consider possible adjacencies.

After months of discussion, we name the gathering *Our Trails Bring Us Together*. The present tense here is, of course, no accident.

As conference planning reaches fever pitch, Bancroft Library refuses to loan us the maps. Why? They say our security systems are subpar. (We demonstrate otherwise.) They say our archival, climate-control systems are subpar. (We demonstrate otherwise.) They say the maps would have to be insured for travel and they cannot be insured because they have never been appraised. (They get appraised.) Now Bancroft Library most certainly will not loan us the maps. It appears they are very valuable.

We contend that the maps' monetary value is nothing compared to the cultural meaning they hold for us. For the First Nations and Alaska Native peoples whose lands and ancestors infuse it, for all Yukon-Alaska inhabitants, Indigenous and migrant alike, who live in the cross-cultural world descended from those maps' making, for knowledge makers and knowledge seekers across disciplines, searching through history, language, even the stars themselves, for more traction, one hair at a time, in the slick sheen of continual expansion stretching our universe end to impossible end.

August 8, 2019

Director, Bancroft Library
University of California Berkeley

Dear Ms.——,

We are writing to express our deep concern that the Bancroft Library has not yet confirmed a decision to loan the original Kohklux and Kandik maps for display at our events planned for October 2019.

We are hosting a series of international gatherings in the North with descendants of the map creators to commemorate the 150th anniversary of their drawing. The original maps are the focal point of all our events. It will be a once in a lifetime opportunity for our Elders, our Indigenous Language Speakers, and—most crucially—for our youth to experience firsthand the powerful knowledge, strength, and artistic talent of our ancestors.

Most Alaskans and Yukon people would never be able to travel to California to see these maps. Our event is thus designed to provide an irreplaceable opportunity to witness the maps' extraordinary representations of our landscapes and our languages—in person.

However, we are now just two months away from our opening dates and still have no confirmation of Bancroft's loan. Yet our Coordinating Committee has been communicating with Bancroft Library for over a year. We have offered information, contacts, and data to assist them. We have sent dozens of emails and letters providing detailed descriptions of our events, our organizations, and our facilities. We have participated in numerous phone calls.

We appreciate that the loan of these original documents requires tremendous amount of analysis, time and effort. And we appreciate that your staff must consider all necessary precautions for safe transport and display of these precious heritage resources. Bancroft's lack of confirmation remains alarming.

Please consider that we receive many shipments of irreplaceable cultural and artistic pieces for display every year. We take our commitments to preservation and security with the utmost care. No one is more concerned than we are to ensure that these archival records are preserved for all future time. We know that we will contribute unique and irreplaceable intellectual and cultural information to assist the Bancroft Library and people worldwide in valuing and understanding these maps.

In this UNESCO year of recognition for Indigenous Languages and the people like us who preserve them as world heritage resources, we are concerned that our efforts to celebrate these maps in our homelands may fail. It would be extremely unfortunate if one of the critical messages emerging from our events was that the Bancroft Library would not permit the original maps to be displayed in the North where they were created and where they have the most enduring connections and significance for all future generations.

Please provide us with an immediate response to our loan request so that we may finalize our plans for school tours, public presentations, advertising, and all the many other aspects of our events.

Thank you on behalf of all our people,

XXX

XXX

XXX

Bancroft relents. They will loan us one but not the other. The small map. The one frustrated by scale.

On this condition: they say it must be accompanied by a Californian chaperone. They say the map and chaperone must be picked up from the airport in Vancouver. We indicate that there is an international airport in Whitehorse, which is preferable, because Vancouver is a four-day drive away. What? they say. Unthinkable. Distances that vast do not exist. We assure them that, in fact, the North is full of distances, but not to worry, because of that airport we mentioned, the one right here, which will save everyone the trouble of a four-day drive to and from Vancouver. What's this? they say. Distances that vast exist?

Why? What are they for, such distances? Decisively, they stomp their feet: nowhere has ever been that far from anything else in the entire universe of California. We blink.

Ultimately Bancroft Library sends a chaperone to Whitehorse with a single sheet of paper. Her job is to guard it from us. She places it in a glass box and we are permitted to talk about it. She is very pleasant.

Our gathering, remember, carries this name: *Our trails bring us together.*

V. THE CONFERENCE

Not *brought*, but *bring*. Bessie Cooley, Inland Tlingit Elder from Teslin, explains the choice of present tense. *"Our trails* bring *us together" has a more extensive meaning because it's ongoing*, she says. *It has that meaning of action. On the part of the* trails.

It begins with Tlingit dancers in full regalia. Klukwan's Lani Hotch, Jack Strong, and Marsha Hotch. They fill Whitehorse's Kwanlin Dün Cultural Centre with drumbeats, voice, dance. The drums pound, our hearts pound, and the air, perhaps it pounds too. Either way, it holds us up. It always does.

Between songs, Lani Hotch speaks. She says, *We're all here together for a few days. And we need to prepare our hearts for what's to come.*

What *is* to come? The 1869 eclipse will reach totality in Klukwan. The furs will be traded in Fort Selkirk. The trail will be traveled. Again, and again, and again. One day—a section of the trail will even be paved. We call it the Haines Highway. Or the Haines Cut-Off. (Truly, paved or not, that trail is the only way through those mountains.) But what, exactly, *is* to come?

Speeches. Panels. Q and As. An art installation. Tea. Soup, cookies, tablecloths draping round tables.

A tap of the microphone, a brightening of the stage lights. *These maps weren't for us*, says Steve Smith, chief of the Champagne-Aishihik First Nations. *These maps are for those of you who would get lost.*

Or, in Champagne-Aishihik First Nations Elder Ron Chambers's words, *they were people who knew how to find their way up here. They didn't need a map. Their language was their map. Davidson came, and* he *needed a map. They were able to make one for him.*

Or, in former territorial archivist Linda Johnson's words, Linda who found the maps in the eighties, Linda whose life shifted with that discovery, *We have to temper our excitement and awe that we have for these maps with some of the reality that: Tlingit ancestors had all that information in their heads, and carried it around with them everywhere they went.*

Yes. Says the archivist, whose passion and profession is the preservation and study of documents, the archivist who found *the* Kohklux Map in Bancroft Library's own archives, the archivist who held this beautiful sheet of paper in her own hands, whose eyes still glisten as tears spring toward the memory of that moment. *That is the more impressive archive. What people carried in their minds.*

VI. WHAT'S TO COME

For myself, this is what I see: a density of pencil lines and a storm of finely shaded detail. An eye-bending level of detail. Mountain peaks and ridgelines cast against empty sky, or against blank distance, I don't know. Mountains portrayed from a valley perspective looking up. Rivers and lakes traced in bird's-eye view, from a ridgeline perspective looking down.

The mapmakers saw clearly. Clearly the timbre of the voices of their ancestors. Clearly the contours of generations to come. Clearly the turns of the forested land, clearly the shape of the sinuous lakesides, clearly the jags of every ridgeline against every sky.

Cubism, I think, though I calculate the mapmakers drew this map two generations before Picasso. Indeed, the map multiplies points of view, hybridizes lines of sight. Viewers see the world at hand from different angles simultaneously, and in different ways.

Now and again, I ask people what they make of this. We shake our heads. No one can say.

Then one day, I ask Tom Buzzell.

Tom Buzzell sleeps in Haines Junction. Tom has stood in many, many of the places depicted on the map. *We have thousands of mental pictures gathered into one place*, he reflects. *It's a download of what was going on in their minds that day*. Tom is a member of Champagne-Aishihik First Nations, inland Tlingit groups close kin of the coastal Tlingits from Klukwan in Jilk̲aat Aani and beyond. And Tom works as First Nations liaison officer for the Kluane National Park and Reserve. For Tom, the map is both personal and professional.

I ask Tom what he makes of the mingling. The points of view. The perspective from the sky looking down enmeshed with the perspective of the land looking up. Why are they doing cubism? Why do they need more than one perspective at once in order to see what they see? What does clarity—perceptually—require of us?

You look where you're going next, Tom says.

What he means is that as you pick your way along the riverbank, you keep your eyes up. You scan the mountain you will ascend. In the high country, you look down and out. You memorize the contours of lakeshores and waterways you'll cross after your descent. You look where you're going next because you can see it better from a distance. Once you're there, you rely on the memory of what you've seen. And you keep looking ahead.

Time is like that. So says this map. Memory guides us through the present and from the present we must look to the future, memorize it as best we can, hold close our memories of what will be.

It reminds me of words featured on the conference banners. One banner quotes Tagish Elder Clara Schinkel who asks, in 1994, "How are we going to know where we are going if we don't know where we came from?" She explains: "This map really means a lot to us because it shows us the trail our ancestors used to come into the Yukon." Memory is a landmark for the future.

The mapmakers drew every day of a monthlong journey with a consciousness of movement, with anticipation for sustained travel. In other words, they've mapped a state of being: one of continual preparation for what's to come. One of looking forward—of reading, and so charting, the future.

VII. THE MAPMAKERS' POLITICAL MOMENT

European and American explorers sailed into the region in the mid-1700s. By the 1800s, Russia had claimed Alaska. It set to work exploiting its fur resources, a large-scale economic project that entailed a degree of business cooperation—and a degree of violent conflict—with coastal Tlingits.

Around the same time, British fur traders expanded overland through North America. They tapped into the interior Yukon fur trade and established a Hudson's Bay Company (HBC) post at Fort Selkirk.

This did not sit well with the Chilkat Tlingit. They had a total trade monopoly on southern and central Yukon until the British HBC moved in.

The historically recorded details of Kaalaxch's life begin here. In 1852, Kaalaxch' and his father Skeetl'aka traveled from Klukwan into the interior. They led a raid on the HBC post at Fort Selkirk. No one was injured. But their attack drove the HBC out of Yukon. It effectively reestablished the Chilkat as the sole gatekeepers to trade in the interior. The Chilkat Tlingit won.

So it is that we may do well to think of Kaalaxch's life as one spent continually contending with powerful and volatile outside forces. So it is that we may do well to think of Kaalaxch's life as one spent in continual delicate negotiation, cultivating/refining/fighting to conduct trade on his people's terms, and navigating international power struggles in the local, Alaska-Yukon space of tumultuous cross-cultural politics.

In 1867, fifteen years after the raid on Fort Selkirk, Russia abruptly sold Alaska to the US. The Russians, with whom Kaalaxch' had negotiated for so long, simply left. And the Americans arrived. Kaalaxch' very suddenly had to create new relationships with new outside powers entirely. Kaalaxch' very suddenly had to contend with a new culture; with new figureheads of power who spoke a different language.

It was a pivotal moment, says Linda Johnson of the era in which Kaalaxch' and Davidson met one another, traveled together, and formed their relationship. Linda goes on:

> It is the time when the interior of Yukon is *about* to be, as they say, opened up like a can. And it's the time when everything's about to change in Klukwan. Real lifestyle change is going to take a few more years. However the power struggles have already begun, the booze is already pouring in, and opportunities to participate in another culture and another economy are enlarging daily.

And what about North America writ large? When this backdrop pulls focus, we see the creation and gifting of the Kohklux Map occurs during a period in which Colonial British, Canadian, and American national policy toward Indigenous people centers on one thing: aggressive assimilation.

Historian Thomas King, in his book *The Inconvenient Indian*, explains the era's attitude toward Indigenous North Americans. The US Supreme Court's 1823 *Johnson v. McIntosh* decision, for example, confirmed that all land in the boundaries of the United States belonged to the federal government by right of discovery: Native people had the right of occupancy but did not hold legal title to their lands. In a second example, when the Cherokee tried to argue that they were a foreign nation and therefore not subject to the laws of Georgia, the 1831 *Cherokee v. Georgia* decision determined that Native people were not sovereign but rather domestic, dependent nations. "With these decisions," writes King, "all Indian land within America now belonged to the federal government."

And with the US purchase of Alaska, Kaalaxch's people (and many, many others) also, technically, belonged to the US federal government.

And that government designed and executed policy—such as the 1830 US Indian Removal Act—with the explicit intent to exterminate Indigenous North American people and cultures.

King invokes tribe after tribe after tribe; nation after nation after nation. The Shawnee. The Ottawa. The Wyandot. The Creek, the Chickasaw, the Cherokee, the Seminole, the Potawatomi, Sauk and Fox, Osage, Kickapoo, Ho-Chunks, Kaskaskia, Peoria, Miami, Delaware, Illinois, Modoc, Oto, Ponca, Seneca, Cayuga, Tuskegee, and Quapaw. "These are," writes King, "the names of a few tribes that were removed from their homelands during the middle of the nineteenth century." And King is quick to note what the list entirely omits: that the upheavals of removal policy "in many cases broke the back of the communities."

Later in 1865, the US abolished slavery. But it continued to deny Indigenous people virtually all citizenship rights.

King's *Inconvenient Indian* is just as critical of Canadian policy. It's a couple decades behind the US but makes virtually all the same moves, formalizing "an identical relationship with Native people" with the 1867 passage of the Indian Act.

That is when Kaalaxch' welcomed the American George Davidson into his Chilkat homeland: several decades into US Indian "removal," at the dawn of Canadian Indian "relocation." At a time when, as King says: "It was official. Indians in all of North America were property."

I think suddenly of Tom Buzzell with his eyes on the map. He said that *good places to stop are good places to stop*. He was talking about campsites, the necessity of rest during long travel, of replenishment—but with *The Inconvenient Indian* on the mind, I think of metaphoric stopping places too. I think of everyone in all of time who has ever woken up in the morning and gone out into the day and put an end to something.

Good places to stop are good places to stop, said Tom Buzzell. *You find those places by following trails*. That is one reason to follow a trail others have taken before: It will lead you to necessary refuge. In my mind, I also rehear Bessie Cooley's voice: *It has that meaning of action. On the part of the* trails.

On the banks of the milky frigid waters of the Chilkat River, Kaalaxch', Tu_eek, and Kaatchxich spent three days penciling one such trail as a gift for their guest, George Davidson. Then Davidson toiled mightily alongside his hosts, inscribing the map with myriad words in myriad languages he did not know.

Sometimes cultures meet and mingle and instead of bloodshed, something beautiful comes of it. Like a map.

Of North America's social struggles today, Linda Johnson says, *We're trying to find the balance—for reconciliation*. And without a beat, she continues: *The trails are always there. It's just a question of how deeply they're buried.*

I think of this, the merging of trail and society. The merging of map and ethics, travel and relationship. Peace—at any time, and between any people—is precious. Peace is so, so precious. Have you witnessed it before? Peace?

Sometimes, I think that I have.

Sometimes, I don't know if I have, but I still think maybe I will.

Here is this essay's thesis: Our inheritance from the past is entangled not only with projects of extermination but also of peace. Instances of trust, generosity, creativity, and cooperation also had a hand, however quietly, in creating us as we now are.

VIII. THINGS WE IMAGINE

I will travel soon. It is fall, nearly winter. Our great gathering is over. People danced, drumbeats pounded the air, voices spun through hallways and leapt across floors and sallied across crisp, white tablecloths. Entire knowledge systems looked one another in the eye and burst out laughing, sudden friends. Trails converged.

But now it is time for me, like so many others, to go home. From Whitehorse the dog and I will drive through a hundred miles of boreal forest west to Haines Junction, where we will turn left—south. We'll take the Haines Highway 150 miles to the beach. First it will take us up into the alpine and over the mountains and through the same pass Kaalaxch' walked so many times. Then the road will drop steeply into the mossy rainforests of my coastal roots. The road will flatten in the Chilkat Valley and run alongside those milky frigid waters I've been thinking about. After 120 miles on the Haines Highway, we'll pass the cutoff to Klukwan. Another thirty miles on the road will get us to the Haines ferry terminal. I'll drive the truck onto the ferry, haul my sleeping bag up to the solarium and hunker down for the day as the ferry motors seventy-five miles down Lynn Canal to my hometown, which is ringed by an icefield and leashed by no road at all. When the ferry docks in Auke Bay, I'll get back in the truck, drive off the ferry, turn right—southeast—and the dog and I will travel the last seventeen miles home. The rain may float about in feathery distraction or spit like needles or simply splat on this and that in its clownish, silver way. Homeward bound, my heart always looks toward the face of the rain.

What I'm winding around to in my mind is the possibility that home includes *the way home*.

As one part preparation for travel and one part farewell, I sit down to chat with Linda one last time. We are both deeply tired and deeply warmed by the gathering. But as we get to talking, we get to time traveling, going *in* to the Kohklux Map.

Linda imagines arriving as a newcomer into the Jilk̲aat Tlingits' homeland. *If you were George Davidson and others coming up the Chilkat [River Valley] for the first time, all you see is a wall of mountains*, she says. She faces me across a small square table, sponged surface only lightly sticky. *All you see is a wall of mountains*, she says. *The route goes through that barrier—in a very precise way.*

Because I know I will pass through the place, Klukwan, that Linda is talking about I make a mental note to pause when I get there, let the dog out, and look upvalley. I make a mental note to look from Klukwan toward Yukon and to think of outsiders, of guests, of first-timers facing serious topography. I make a mental note to imagine them contemplating a wall of mountains, considering the journey they either want to undertake or want to be able to undertake, a journey unimaginable without cooperation with keen minds and skills of those who know. Call it friendship?

And so several days later, in Klukwan, I stand on the banks of the frigid and milky waters of the Chilkat River. I face that upvalley wall, face those mountains. November sun blazes in the north wind. It rockets down the valley off the snowfields up in the pass, makes quick work burning my cheeks. The dog touches my leg once, very softly. She suggests we keep moving.

Later, in Klukwan's Heritage Center, I read, "Those mountains were our fence posts." Tlingits of Klukwan were responsible for everything they could see from the banks of the Chilkat River all the way through the forest and up that wall of mountains.

I chat softly with Lani Hotch, one of the three Klukwan dancers who opened the conference, the one who had said, *We must prepare our hearts for what's to come*. Lani is an Elder and culture bearer and serves as the Jilḵaat Ḵwáan Heritage Center curator and cultural education specialist.

Yes, she confirms, those mountains are their fence posts. Her people are responsible for everything they can see from here all the way up that wall of mountains. But they traveled far beyond their own lands, remember. *Our ancestors were so fit*, Lani says. *Our ancestors walked everywhere*.

Those mountains were the fence posts beyond which Lani's people traveled as powerful guests. They left their territory, they traversed territories belonging to others, they walked very, very far, approaching other peoples' campfires, trading and bartering the contents of heavy, heavy packs. And those who knew the way across those mountains, those who knew the way inland—their knowledge ran deep, deep. Much clearer than the milky waters of the Chilkat River seasonally swollen with hooligans. Much, much clearer.

That is why Headman Kaalaxch' and his wives, Tu_eek and Kaatchxich, were able to draw it.

IX. LINEAGE

I cannot shake the feeling that what happens in places stays there, rinsing over those of us who pass through.

We curate the public face of history, of course. But is it possible that we inherit as much from the lesser-told and untold stories as the repeated ones?

Danica Boice, a folklorist from northern, rural British Columbia, points out that our wider culture's most-repeated histories center on stories of destruction, wartime, famine, fleeing, and force. Western narrative theory even tries to convince us that without conflict, there is no story. But, argues Boice, between its periods of conflict and bloodshed, the global history of the human animal is highly cooperative and rhythmic. Specifically, most of human history consists of repetitive labor punctuated by periods of relaxation. Deeply embedded in the species' ancestral inheritance, Boice emphasizes, are the simple, sustaining rhythms of shared labor and rest.

The Kohklux Map, I believe, offers a local line of sight into what Boice is getting at. It maps the land, but it also maps out a long lineage of cooperation, hard work, and rest.

Alongside its land-based specificity, the map offers an expansive take on where we came from—and therefore also on where we are going. Where we came from, where we are going, and where along the way are some good places to stop.

I wonder what the three Tlingit mapmakers thought about as they pulled pencils across paper. I wonder what they thought about as their guests stood by, perhaps idle, or perhaps busy with this and that, preparing their instruments and notebooks for the day the sun would go out, and then come back on, inside an unflinching universe that, presumably, kept expanding all the while.

X. SIDEBAR

Many published histories—including Davidson's own article, published in 1901—erroneously state that Headman Kaalaxch', Tu_eek, and Kaatchxich drew the large map *after* the solar eclipse darkened the Chilkat Valley.

But recent close readings of Davidson's diaries indicate that the trio drew the map *before* the eclipse. The diaries demonstrate that Davidson was already working to transcribe the place names provided by the three mapmakers in the days leading up to the eclipse.

It is telling that Davidson—and historians who followed—altered the chronology of events.

They've reordered it as such: the eclipse, the darkness, the reappearance of the sun, the drawing of the map. So arranged, adjacency implies three Tlingit leaders shared their coveted knowledge because the Americans made the sun reappear.

Of course the Americans did not make the sun reappear. The Americans were just watching the universe expand, along with everyone else. Which, incidentally, is probably happening all the time whether anyone watches or not.

But we may do well to recognize that from Montezuma to Kaalaxch', Western history often dramatizes moments of awe among Indigenous peoples. Coupled with a tendency to downplay stories of Indigenous self-determination, this pattern in the historic record plays a devious hand in building wider and widening complacencies.

In the case of the Kohklux Map, let us simply be forthright. Headman Kaalaxch' and his wives, Tu_eek and Kaatchxich, drew a map for George Davidson. We don't really know why. It's a map that looks to where it's going next. It's a map that speaks to yearly, seasonal trade rhythms, to daily travel rhythms, and to the simple necessity of neighbors working together. It's a map not of boundaries or borders but of shapes and shades: the shapes of ancient meeting grounds, the shades of topography. It charts not divisions but rather momentum itself. I have seen nothing like it before or since.

Those maps depict the space-between as a fullness in itself. They prove the space-between to be the generative center.

What happens between us, I mean to say, is the most important.

XI. THE MEDICINE

"We live permanently," writes Michael Ondaatje, "in the recurrence of our own stories, whatever story we tell."

Here, then, is a story I want to tell.

A mountain range runs nearly four thousand miles along the western edge of North America. Its northern reach lies in the center of the universe. That's where a raven or a crow, depending on who you ask, made the land, brought the light, and played his tricks. Still does.

Up there, boreal forests lean into those mountains from the East.

Rainforests lean into them from the West.

So it is that beneath peaks and summits, knobby carpets of spiny dripping crackling forests skirt mountain slopes, running all along the northern reach of the northwestern edge of the continent, buttressing those rocky peaks so that they reach right into the belly of the sky, which is the universe, which, according to some, is best understood as a thing in motion. Expanding.

Sometimes entire generations of people lean into each other too, over time and distance. Lean in shoulder to shoulder. Lean in arm in arm, gopher robes shushing along the leaves of Labrador tea. What are they doing, all those people leaning in, elbows linked, laughing without a sound? Holding up mountains, I suppose. So that rocks may always rise higher than vegetation can grow, digging face-first in to the belly of the wind, and find within it only air.

THE ASH AND THE LITERATURE

A Diptych

I. THE ASH

Twelve hundred years ago a volcano exploded and a cloud of molten ash went into the sky. It made a home there.

Perhaps the ash lived in a house of sunbeams. Perhaps it harvested daylight like berries. Perhaps it wove baskets from the sun's warmth to carry all the brimming light that it plucked and gathered from the sky. Either way, using all that sunlight, the cloud of ash cast a long shadow. It chilled the boreal forest to its core.

Of course I think of the fungi, the plants, the animals. I think of everyone in the forest who breathes—be it by leaf, gill, or lung. But I also wonder: What was it like for the cloud of ash to leave the red-black densities deep underground and explode into a cold spacious sky? What would you or I have done, thus catapulted?

People still tell stories about the chill that set in. The year of two winters.

It happened like this. A single bird turned its head to face the far-off oceans. A west wind blew. A volcano erupted. Ash rocketed skyward. The volcano spewed, the wind carried the ash, the sky darkened, the forests cooled. The bird ruffled its feathers. Prepared for a long wait, a deep dive.

The caribou left. The people did too. But not gravity. Gravity stayed put, singing something quiet. The cloud, once molten rock, now cooled to motes of dust. And as it cooled it rode the west wind across its sunstruck home in the sky, throwing a long shadow across the land.

In the end, the cloud of ash spread into the shape of a single tear. Since I believe in geometry, in the power of shape, I think about that. Though it was adrift and made of dust, perhaps the cloud of ash still remembered its old fluidity, the red-black underground of its molten origins.

While it tried to make the best of this new life in the aqueous atmosphere, the cloud of ash eventually heard gravity's quiet song. Straining to place the melody, the cloud squinted. It shut out the bright light of the sky, sensing an unavoidable significance lay inside the tune.

That is when and how the ash began to settle out in its long, earthly return. Mote by mote, ash blanketed the cold earth in a thousand-mile swath of tephra. The ash fell quietly, of course. It filled the air peacefully, like snowflakes. From outer space, the cloud looked like a great ashen tear. It settled out over the forest in the shape of a single, vast droplet.

"The immediate consequences," says anthropologist John Ives, "even if they were brief, would have been quite severe."

I imagine a human hand tensing. Palm pressed to the throwing board, thumb wrapping it firmly, atlatl as extension of the hunter's body, expression of the hunter's conviction. A hand that whitens into sure and sudden grip when all becomes movement and momentum, shoulder and elbow and wrist and an arcing swoop to a final snap, dart flying so hard and fast it plunges through fur, pierces skin, punctures lung or throat. The human hand would pulse in the following moments, adrenaline blooming fast and sharp, atlatl smooth and firm, a tool holding the hand of the hunter as much as that hand holds its tool.

But the year of two winters would have been different. In the year of two winters, a tear-shaped cloud blocked the sun and ash fell like snow. And after that, no one in the boreal forests of southern Yukon made or used atlatls ever again.

The ash that fell like snow was, as geologists specify, obsidian. It blanketed the land in microscopic shards of glass. A dust of razors. All edge, no blade.

At its westernmost reach, at the edge of what's now called the Northwest Territories' Great Slave Lake, a half inch of ash lay as a pale bedsheet on the earth. But in the East, close to what's now the Alaska-Yukon border and the site of the explosion, the ash, snow-like, piled knee-deep. Deeper still where it drifted in the relentless wind. Did it also pile up on spruce boughs until the limbs bent with the weight of powdered stone and glass, shedding in puffs onto drifting dunes of more ash below? Did caribou kick their hooves, sending up gray-white clouds as they waded through, migrating out?

Biologists say that caribou, moose, sheep, and goats suffered dental wear and corneal abrasion. They suffered rumen blockage (from tephra ingestion). They suffered silicosis (respiratory damage from inhaling ash). So great was the volcanic disturbance that it bears a full name—the White River Ash event. Or among technical experts, the WRAe.

Say the archaeologists: southern Yukon's Nabesna and Ahtna neighbors living in Alaska's mountains to the west shifted from hunting with atlatls to hunting with bows and arrows many generations before the ash event. So did their Inuit neighbors to the north. So did their Tlingit neighbors along the coast. Atlatl and dart technology persists in the boreal forests of southern Yukon's archaeologic record longer than in any surrounding ones. It persists right up until the ash fall, at which point bows and arrows replace atlatls completely.

"Did the WRA event play a role in the transition?" Yukon archaeologist Christian Thomas writes, addressing my inquiry. "Probably. But I imagine the transition was inevitable all the same. In my mind the better question is 'Why did southern Yukon folks hold on to dart technology for so long, when they were surrounded by, and trading with, folks who had adopted the arrow?'"

In another email thread, Alberta archaeologist Todd Kristensen chimes in. "I don't think you witness a technology like [bows and arrows] and then try to make it yourself. It's too complicated. I think it's a technological system that has to be learned with guidance. That means it would probably move among people with peaceful relations."

Regarding the persistence of atlatl technology in southern Yukon, Thomas surmises this is a clue about the hunting culture's conservative nature. People may have chosen to hold onto a well-understood technology that gave them more certainty hunting on lean lands, in hungry forests.

Of the sudden shift to bows and arrows, Kristensen advances a theory. Perhaps when ash fell across the inland boreal forest, its people migrated to the coast, seeking refuge in the rainforest among their coastal kin. Perhaps coastal Tlingit people received their inland Southern Tutchone neighbors warmly, sheltering them, integrating them into families, hunting and fishing and foraging all together. Perhaps with a generation of peaceful cohabitation and collaboration, inland boreal forest people became accomplished archers, practicing for many years with their kin on the coast. Perhaps, after the ash event drove everyone out, a new generation of the land's own inhabitants returned home. Still themselves, still inland boreal forest people. But no longer dart hunters. Now archers.

But, the theory goes, not everyone returned home.

Say the linguists: Look at the pockets of Dene language speakers living far, far from Yukon and Alaska. Look at the pockets of Dene speakers who are at home in the deserts of North America's Southwest. Look at the Dene speakers of the Arizona, New Mexico, Texas, and Mexico borderlands. Why is the Dene language family distributed in this way?

Kristensen suggests certain inland boreal forest people sheltering among their coastal kin might have found and filled a niche on the coast mediating peaceful trade.

Who knows. I am no arbiter.

But as Kristensen's theory holds, perhaps southern Yukon people's great social role—their art—was in negotiating. They may have become a kind of merchant class with expertise in brokering trade between other groups. And if this is so, perhaps they continued migrating and liaising. Perhaps their descendants carried this forward across time and space, holding peace between neighbors and migrating all the way to the continent's southwest deserts, where now the descendants of their descendants dwell among stony mountains and life-giving arroyos and breathe air so dry you can hear the sound of a yucca blooming from one valley to another.

In other words, perhaps it was the warp and weft of interreliance that drew Dene language speakers out from under the catastrophic ash fall, guiding them to shelter with trusted neighbors on the coast. Perhaps certain among their descendants then retraced those steps, migrating back into their northern boreal forests, while others extended that southern migration deep into the heart of the continent, all the way into the deserts of the American Southwest, where today a razor-sharp division lashes the land right to itself, all edge and no blade, as the US-Mexico border.

In the North, the White River Ash fall is both event and material. It is both a pivotal time in history as well as a bone-white layer in the sediment strata. Unmistakable. Spot it from a canoe on the upper Yukon River, a milky vein traced high in the sandy banks. Spot it overhead as you walk the narrow footpath along Schwatka Lake looking for swallow nests pocked high into the clay cliffs. Spot it in roadcuts along the Alcan, the crumbly road that tumbles the whole way from one end of southern Yukon to the other and deep into Alaska.

Spot the White River Ash event where you will in any cross section of this life because the truth is that time always lies underfoot. Its bulk has been holding us up all along. And that depth itself may offer a balm, a respite from failure. We are, after all, the kind of animal that likes to think there is always room inside the earth to bury one more wrong.

II. THE LITERATURE

Experts estimate that it takes ten years of training to develop proficient archery skills. For a hunting society to make that shift, they must either have the human capital to excuse certain hunters for a decade-long apprenticeship—or they must inhabit such a rich environment that their hunters can afford low success rates during a decade-long learning curve. The inland, boreal forest people of southern Yukon had neither. Atlatl technology worked well. Too well to gamble.

But a generation of cohabitation with their coastal neighbors in lush, dark rainforests edging rich, salty beaches would have changed both circumstances. There would have been the time, the community, and the plenitude to study, learn, practice, hone.

This weekend I drive from Yukon over the pass into Alaska and sleep in a tent by the sea. Seaside, rainforested Alaska is where I was born, where my family lives. Inland, boreal-forested Yukon is where I spend a year "abroad," among our Canadian neighbors. More and more, as I move among those neighbors, I see my sense of home incorporates them, takes its shape from their proximity.

I wake up inside my purple tent and pet the dog for a long time. Later, I film the incoming tide on the mudflats; no reason, just enthralling. I watch sea lions cartwheel, listen to barnacles combing their wavelets. I feed the dog her kibbles. And then I pack up, drive back toward Canada. But I stop in the high country. Kill the engine. Put on my snowshoes. I am in White Pass, between Carcross, Yukon and Skagway, Alaska. Somewhere in the North American borderlands, snowshoeing aimlessly, excellent dog at my side.

The sun strikes hard. The snow strikes back. My sunglasses are too flimsy for the way snow multiplies light. Around me the peaks, too, are sharp, and I wonder at the people in far cities so many years ago, people in Moscow and London or some such, those who thought these mountains were a good place to make a line between nations. To divide and delineate the world.

I consider the vast distances, physical and non, between this border as compared to the southern one. This border: the one that underlies the April snowpack on the spine of a northern mountain range across which ancient people fled ancient ash. And that one: the border occupying national news every day, the one that crosses the desert of North America's Southwest. Impossible to think of anything else, after all. It is 2019, the year that the US locks children in cages. The dog blinks, tilts her nose upward.

I have been reading the work of Francisco Cantú. He asks that when we consider the US-Mexico border we think of home. He asks that when we consider those who cross it, we think of those we hold dear.

The dog and I stand in a cageless borderlands. A cageless borderlands that has always been a borderlands—between Southern Tutchone and Tlingit, between boreal forest and rainforest, eons and eons of cagelessness etched into the air itself. I breathe, perceive sun blaring, slopes pounding, sky droning. I perceive silence in other words, silence seared with the overwhelm of spring sunshine gutting winter from the land as if the whole long season were a single fish belly to slit and empty out onto the rocks.

Francisco Cantú was a border patrol agent. He enforced the law up and down and back and forth across the desert, trying to give water to people who were thirsty, people he trapped because he was paid to—people he trapped, yet also cared for because he is perceptive, human. Certain among us can be like that. Some put their fingers right into the wound itself, use their own lives trying to stanch the flow loosed by larger problems. They may end up with blood on their hands, teetering at the edge of being able to live with themselves. Those of us who hold to our silences must envy their courage. Anyhow, Francisco Cantú wrote a book about all this. *The Line Becomes a River*.

It is springtime, April when I stand in these northern borderlands, snowshoes on my feet, shining black dog by my side. By June that same year, the US Immigration and Customs Enforcement agency will be holding about thirteen thousand children apprehended from similar borderlands, southern ones.

The numbers from June 2019 resemble those from 1879 to 1918 when the US government took twelve thousand children from their parents and their nations and put them into the Carlisle Indian School, the institution on which hundreds of federally funded, church-run boarding schools across North America's Canada and US were ultimately modeled.

History is like that. Always happening now.

Now.

In fact as I write this essay, news breaks of an unmarked graveyard found at the residential school in Kamloops, BC, and 215 children's remains buried in it. Some public personalities express shock: buried children! What horrible secrecy! But the rebuke is swift. Every family who lost a child knew full well they lost a child. Every single one was missed, and has been missed, by entire communities who have known all along precisely who returned from residential school and precisely who did not.

A few months later, news breaks again. This time, an estimated 751 unmarked graves. This time, at Marieval in Saskatchewan.

Then, schools. Now, cages. Does time pass? Does any time, ever, pass? The Puritan poet Anne Bradstreet writes,

"Everything you do has already been done. Everything you say has already been said."

Someone else, though I don't recall who, writes, "An unmarked grave is always unmarked for a reason."

It seems the earth holds us, and in more ways than one. It holds our living bodies as well as our dead. It holds our pasts; it holds our futures. It props open the distances between us and solidifies our proximities to one another.

I think of the people who fled the ash fall, the people who crossed borders and whose neighbors welcomed them. I think of the ones who became archers and then returned home—still themselves, yet changed by skill, by muscle memory, by careful study, close tutelage. And I think of their maybe-relatives, relatives across generations of time and a continent's worth of distance, language relatives dwelling along the southern border. A border across which various other neighbors now face one another from behind bars, cage doors poised. What would it take for us to welcome, rather than cage, people seeking refuge today?

Let us consult the archaeologists. Writes Kristensen: "A butchered bison leaves bones behind; a fur trade post leaves rotting walls for archaeologists to discover. But humans are more than what we eat and build. To many, our lives are defined by relationships to other people."

And let us consult the literature. Some twelve hundred years ago, during the White River Ash event, it is true that the earth exploded and that in the end, everyone with feet and wings migrated out from beneath the great cloud of ash that descended onto the land in the shape of a single tear.

Every map I have ever seen shows it as such. As droplet-shaped. As a 130,000-square-mile deposition curving from eastern Alaska's Wrangell-Saint Elias Mountains across all of southern boreal-forested Yukon right into the Northwest Territories to meet with the shores of Great Slave Lake.

But to be precise, that strange and confident tear-shaped geometry does have a blemish, a single inconsistency in its curve. And that is the lakeshore itself. At the hard, undeniable edge of the earth, where true waves crash against a true beach, the White River Ash deposition goes jaggedly unmapped.

A TRIANGLE OF SUN

I smell permafrost again today. We pull it up from under the bog. We drill under, pull up, and breathe in.

It starts like this: the full-stop thunk of a probe clunking into the frost layer. Then the corer clangs, dried with ancient muds. Makes a round, black borehole in the sphagnum bog.

And in the end, there is the sound of the permafrost core dropping back into the hole—hollow, clunk, wet. When will its margins refreeze? When will its center melt out? What time, really, is it?

Geologists organize the earth's calendar. They say the Quaternary Period comprises this past 2.6 million years. It begins with the onset of Northern Hemisphere glaciation. It continues as the Ice Age. Glaciation extends from the poles as far as forty degrees latitude. Anatomically modern humans evolve. Speciation yields *Homo sapiens*. That is the Quaternary.

I know a permafrost scientist who says, *Ice and humans come into the world together. They live here side by side. They always have.*

Plants, on the other hand, are another kind of animal entirely.

Plants live and die and live and die. Plants die and form inches of peat, and peat doesn't decompose because it is cold, wet, acidic. This can go on a long time. This can all build up. The peat smells old. It smells damp, musty. But it has no odor of rotting, nor of decay. Peat, like most dirt, is clean as can be.

Looking for permafrost in the bog, we pull out a drippy block of surface earth and drill into the peat. We pass around a chunk of it. Cold bolts into my hands. Water runs down my wrist, meets my sleeve. We're out of balance on our dumb stumps, wanting right away to pass the frozen peat to someone else. Our feet sink. They chill in the squish of a bog draped over depths of ancient ice.

People burn this kind of dirt for heat. People burn peat. So I deduce that peat knows the thrill of combustion, the blaze of immediacy. But in the bog, the clock slows. In the bog, a heavy layer of peat insulates underground permafrost from the vagaries of seasons wheeling by above. It's a sopping, seeping blanket, an instrument of deep sleep, topped with flaming mosses.

The silent and the incendiary.
The rapid and the gradual.
The immediate and the continuous.
No one has ever, not once, properly explained these poles.
Surely it's not irrelevant that physicists seem to have dispensed with time entirely.

Yet time lies at the heart of experience. And so the geologists persist. They say the Quaternary Period comprises 2.6 million years. Geologists then divide those 2.6 million years into two epochs: the Pleistocene and the Holocene.

Pleisto-cene. Holo-cene. *Cene* is Greek for *new*. Many geologic epochs end with *cene* and so invoke newness in one way or another—one epoch changes to another and, by definition, change yields something new.

Most of the Quaternary Period's 2.6 million years occur in the Pleistocene. Then, just 11,700 years ago everything changes. And geologists name that particular instance of the ensuing world's alterity "the Holocene."

Holos is the Greek word for *whole*.

Holos + *cene* = wholly new.

My body has softened even as it has moved through many hard places.

Yes, the Holocene is a new world as all the previous epochs have also been new worlds, but the Holocene is not only a *new* world. It is a *wholly new* world. The world as it once was becomes, with the Holocene, an entirely different place.

Because the Holocene encompasses the last ten thousand–plus years of human history, we can surmise the *Holocene* is simply, *the world as we know it*. In contrast to *the world as it once was*.

Soil holds up stories. What lives there? Plants, insects, footsteps.

Soil holds up stories, and so do people. We live now in a wholly new world, but our oldest stories lucidly recall the world as it once was. Our oldest stories even tell us exactly how the world as it once was became the world as we now know it. I learned that from experts, you know.

In my part of the world the stories involve Raven. He's a real nuisance, they say. Amoral instigator of transgression and transformation of the existing order. Someone unpredictable whose behavior has unintended consequences. But the consequences can be cosmic. So the old stories watch that Raven carefully.

Today I watch the spongy wet ground under my boots. I watch the dark wetness climbing my pant legs. The wind reminds me of another time and place in my life. "My" life. My body is changing like the land.

Other parts of the world watch Crow. They watch Coyote and Hermes and Mercury and Loki and Anansi and Eshu. Anthropologists love this: the Trickster *archetype*! they say, clapping their hands. Either way he's a he, and he's cunning and greedy and resourceful, and the world is in large part a product of his caprice.

Which explains the Holocene well enough. The Holocene is the trick that happens when there's a sudden warming, an end to the Pleistocene Epoch. Glacial meltwater surges. Floods swamp the world over.

Approximately all cultures from approximately everywhere recount those floods. Some understand themselves to inhabit a post-disaster social order—this is to say, some still see themselves as descendants of the few who survived the flooding catastrophe. Some see their social systems as those which emerged among people reeling from transformative, fantastic loss. We survive our scars.

We survive, are scars?

Adapted, we call it now. *With resilience*, we say. It means carrying on, with a difference.

Anyhow, no one said the earth ever held still.

Then again, no one said people depend on permanence, either.

Of course the Great Flood is only part of the Holocene. Major extinctions also sweep the globe. From North America for example, horses and camels disappear (though some populations migrate from North America across Beringia into Asia before the waters rise. And the newly Asian camels and horses live on). Mammoths and saber-tooth cats, on the other hand, disappear worldwide.

So goes the interglacial epoch during which the world becomes less icy. So goes the interglacial epoch during which the world becomes more watery. And humans? Rapid proliferation. We skyrocket in scale and scope.

I guess we like it warm. I guess we like it wet. I guess we like it with fewer cats. Whose world is it, after all?

This is what I know from science. This is what I know from living. Barry Lopez counsels:

> If you want to know more about the raven, bury yourself in the desert so that you have a commanding view of the high basalt cliffs where he lives. Let only your eyes protrude. Do not blink. . . . Wait until a generation of ravens has passed away. Of the new generation there will be at least one bird who will find you. He will see your eyes staring up out of the desert floor. . . . Let him have the first word. Be careful: he will tell you he knows nothing.

There it goes: Below has morphed from solid to squish. Alive again.

So be it for the trickster, the force Lewis Hyde calls the "disruptive imagination" that propels the evolutionary trajectories of planetary and cultural systems—and that is also antithetical to the maintenance of those systems.

What kind of animal are we, anyway? A kind that walks on surfaces. Does our best. Does our worst. Wonders at the things beneath, the depths we can't get to without making them into surfaces of their own. A kind of animal that lives atop the bedrock without a compass. A kind of animal that squishes about in a melting bog. That fumbles an ice-hot felted peat core, concerned suddenly with group etiquette over the brown, wet, sloppy surprise of it. That follows the fragrant crush of Labrador tea along the slow curve of melancholy.

My body has more bones than I know. Come sit with me. Look at the land. The shadow of a tree crosses a triangle of sun.

SALSA

I know a man who yearns to eat the sea. Yet he is a human and humans are the kind of animal that cannot really eat the sea. Still, when he thinks no one is watching, he walks to the edge of the tide, kneels, dips his hand into the water and raises it to his mouth. He sips the brine.

I've never seen him close his eyes when he drinks seawater from the cup of his hand, but I know that in the moment he swallows, those pale eyes are looking somewhere far. Somewhere neither of us will get to go. Then he'll stand, purse his mouth, give his wet hand a shake. *Need oysters*, he'll say, and I know he is hungry for the sea. *Need oysters*, he'll say again, nodding, and I know that although he sometimes drinks straight from it, the sea itself cannot feed him.

So he is right to speak of oysters. Oysters are one way for a human animal to swallow the sea.

This is the nature of swallowing: We take in what we do not have. We integrate from without what we cannot create from within. Pulling something of the world into our own depths, we affirm a fundamental porosity between "self" and "surroundings." There is a humbleness to that porosity, and an essential reciprocity, and an expansiveness. Even a fragility.

Recently, I thought of the man who sips the sea. In my mind's eye I saw his stance on the rocks, the cup of his palm, his pursed mouth. His hand's brisk shake and the drops of seawater flung through the air. I saw him because of what happened across my whole tongue when I swallowed a mouthful of kelp and chili and lime and tomato and salt on the curled scoop of a tortilla chip.

With that mouthful of salsa, unexpectedly, the sea flooded in. I tasted an ocean of seawater and smoke. An ocean bloodred with the singed and scorching sun. A dark ocean permeated and dense with savory ash. My throat recognized in this salsa the marine depths an oyster would deliver. I thought of the man who sips the sea.

But take note: A salsa is no oyster. A salsa does not mediate between human animal and the sea.

A salsa mediates between human animal and the sun.

Yes. That seems correct. With salsa we pull equatorial flame straight into our bellies. With crushed and salted tomatoes, with limes, with chili peppers and spices, a salsa feeds us what we do not have, what we cannot create, what we completely require—the sun itself. A salsa is the way a human animal eats sheer light. A salsa is the way a human animal swallows heat.

A salsa is the way a human animal takes in the astral force that makes life possible on this earth.

Life which began, they say, with the smallest of the smallest single cells. Remember them? Adrift. Suspended in seawater filled with light. Imagine life small as an inkling and steady as desire swaying in the water column all day, every day, from then till now.

Here sits a salsa made of kelp. Here sits a merging of sun and sea. And here sits my mind inside my body upon the orbiting planet pondering a jar.

The jar is round.

The label is blue.

White curls cross the label in a sinuous design suggesting movement. Waves in the water, I suppose.

Though the more I ponder the label, the more I perceive those curls as smoke.

Remarkable, I think, to find the ashy density I tasted depicted on the jar itself. It must be the smoke that comes of the sun's daily plunge into the sea. Come close. Hear in the image the nightly hiss of flame meeting water as the sun dips into the horizon's chill waves. Taste the flavor of their mutual joining, the flavor of sun and sea combining into the possibility of life. Shake your hand once, briskly; let drops of seawater fall as they may. Swallow. Watch our planet's watery horizon nightly clasp that ball of fire and see in an instant the mark and measure of all far places we look to in times of reaching, still believing we'll never get to go.

THE END

I ride to the end of the road. A sign marks the place: END ROAD. At the end of the road, I turn around. That is generally what cyclists do on the North Douglas Highway. We ride to the end. Then we turn around.

Early in my Yukon year I acquired a bicycle the color of sea foam. I pedaled up and down sections of the Alcan, learned to handle speed in my descents, learned to climb without losing my cadence. Now my Yukon year is over. Now the dog and I have returned to Alaska. Now this sea foam–colored bike and I speed not down the Alcan, but down the rolling highway that rims the tear-shaped island of my childhood. I speed down the road till it runs out. Then I turn around, making a tight U at the END ROAD sign. As cyclists here do.

The government made that sign. It is a proper yellow sideways square, with a proper black stripe all around it, and black letters in the government's proper roadside size and font.

You know the adage about hiding things in plain sight? END ROAD, says the sign. As if there could be any mistake. So I think about that.

"The past walks through the present," writes Rebecca Solnit, who is also interested in what's hidden in plain sight. "We are ourselves ghosts of other times, not fully present in our own; and we see what is no longer here and feel the future as a wind through the streets, a wind that is for us who look backward always blowing away what we cherish."

This road ends in the trees where the END ROAD sign stands. These trees end in the muskeg, but there is no sign. This muskeg ends in more trees. Those trees end in the beach, which is rocky, and does not end. Yes, there is the sea, and yes, there is its salty froth kicking up steam at the sky, but the beach goes on. It dives down underneath all that.

Though there is, now that I think about it, a sign on the beach. It advises boats not to crash on the rocks. Because, as I said, the beach does not end. Its rocky reef is out there in the water at every tide whether you see it or not. It'll gut your skiff in a second. The beach, then, is marked not because it is an endpoint but because continuity, too, can be treacherous.

On a bicycle my body is also the most continuous continual continuity. On a bicycle my body is concerted rhythm and repetition, cold water crashing on black rocks all day and all night and all moon and all year while the continents shuffle, tectonic adjustments prescient as tea leaves.

I learned to ride a bicycle some decades ago on the paved shoulder of this same highway on this same island. Perhaps you know the place. Not at the end of the road, but out by the boat launch. Where the road peels out of the forest and runs for two miles right alongside the sea, pavement flat and wide and quiet, sky large and cold and crisscrossed by eagles, glacier muscling out of the mountains across the water. I learned to ride a bicycle in that place even though a whale showed up, sending its plumes of breath up into the cold air. I was with my dad, you see. He marveled at the whale. My own focus remained on the bicycle. So I probably learned to balance on two wheels first by exhaling like the whale, loudly, then by requiring my dad to focus on the task at hand, yes, even though a whale, yes, even though the eagles, yes, even though the glacier. That is how I learned to ride a bicycle.

My family laughs about it now. How child-me said: *There's always a whale*. How child-me said: *What I'm trying to do right now is ride a bicycle*.

My grandmother physically startles when I ask her what she remembers of me at my youngest. *You were a ghostly child*, she says.

What a flaming gift, I think, even if I kept my head down for the sake of balance. Abundance breaking the skin of the sea to fill its pliable lungs, abundance slicing the sky with rounded wingtips, abundance muscling its blue-and-white curve between the mountains. And smooth pavement running right through it. Smooth pavement running all the way through to its own abrupt end.

Do you feel bad about that? The pavement running through it? For myself, the answer is dense. I sense that where there is a road—any paved or trafficked road at all—something does, indeed, end.

We are ourselves ghosts of other times. We see what is no longer here.

In a distant and heavily industrialized place, Alberta's Rocky Mountains, scientists have mapped genetically distinct populations of grizzlies, of mountain goats, animals whose habitats are cut by roads and who are stranded in discrete island populations. Populations whose isolation—because they cannot cross the roads—is genetically measurable.

We too live alongside bears and goats. What is the difference between marked ending places and unmarked ones?

The bicycle, of course, permits me to love pavement. Not just to hash out sightlines on my own complicity—to simply, senselessly, love it. Do you understand? I'm saying that flying on pavement flowers my heart straight open.

An ecologist, a professor, and a regulator travel 1,000 miles, 1,500 miles, and 4,000 miles, respectively. But there is no punchline. They travel by invitation to tell a group of us what they, in their heavily paved places, learned of road planning and maintenance and development and design. Their echoes disperse.

Roads beget roads, says the road ecologist. *The world is building roads like crazy*, says the roads professor. *Calcium bedrock is the best indicator for where biodiversity is going to persist into the future*, says the roads regulator. That is what we learn from pavement experts about continuity and transience. Air pushes against the earth and we feel the future as a wind through the streets blowing away what we cherish.

Out North Douglas the pavement at the end of the road is a bit chipped, a bit uneven. There can be loose gravel, loose dogs. In other words, discontinuities abound. Often enough someone wants a photograph with the black-and-yellow government sign. We pose. The government sign—it's basically an old friend, though no one really knows why it's there or what it's really telling us.

One thing hidden in plain sight at the end of the road: a trailhead. It goes to the beach, of course. To raw rock and the salt that pounds it on windy days.

Plate tectonics could be happening right now, this very second. It's hard to tell. I hold my breath. Yes, I hope plate tectonics is happening right now, though it seems the air has gone suddenly still.

Maybe something ends at the end of this road, but it isn't my ride. For my ride, the end is only a halfway mark. In other words, the end of this road is more a time than a place; it's the moment to double down. I make my lollipop turn and fly.

ACKNOWLEDGMENTS

This work is substantially the result of intellectual warmth and friendship extended to me from across cultures and borders. Artists, curators, activists, educators, historians, storytellers, and scientists: I cold-called you without introduction or context, and you responded with the openness and energy that all thinkers, I believe, depend on. Thank you. Errors in this book are my own.

Thank you to the publications that gave early homes to the following pieces:

"Distance Over Light" is a major expansion of the original proto-essay, "Points of Reference," which appeared in *After the Art* (2019).

The earliest version of "The Black Spruce" appeared in a special creative writing issue of *Alaska Magazine* (2019). An excerpt was republished in *Plant Human Quarterly* (2021). A lightly revised version is anthologized in *Rooted2: The Best New Arboreal Nonfiction* (2023) and also appears in the Anchorage Museum's journal, *Chatter Marks* (2024).

"Under the Bridge at Johnson's Crossing" previously appeared in a gallery exhibit and booklet called *Circumpolar*

Duet: Singular Plurality (2020), a collaboration of twenty Yukon-based visual artists and word artists.

"Salsa" was originally published as "The Far Places" by *Edible Alaska* (2020).

"The End" is slightly revised from its original, "The Government Sign," which was anthologized in *Wheels on Ice—Stories of Cycling in Alaska* (2022).

"Chooutla" was first published in *Ploughshares* (2025).

"A Triangle of Sun" and "The Ash and the Literature" were part of an NEH-funded, University of Alaska Fairbanks–organized arts and science collaboration called "In a Time of Change" (ITOC). The text of "A Triangle of Sun" appears in an art book made by Oralee Nudson and figures into the ITOC traveling art exhibit. "The Ash and the Literature" will appear in ITOC's anthology, *Boreal Forest Stories* (2027).

I am grateful to the Fulbright Foundation for funding the research year I spent in Canada's Yukon Territory. Thank you to Yukon University and its Applied Arts Division for hosting my research. Thanks especially to faculty Amanda Graham, Drew Lyness, and Norman Easton for including me in the Yukon University community and to Joanne Lewis for providing access to Yukon University's Institute of Social Justice programs and trainings. This writing also received crucial support from a Rasmuson Foundation Individual Project Award, an Alaska Literary Award, and several grants from the Alaska State Council on the Arts.

Deep gratitude to the Strawberry Committee: readers Caroline Crew, Elizabeth Hall, and Lindsay Webb. Thank you also to readers Leanna Petronella, Erica Watson, Deanna Benjamin, and Mary Odden.

Thank you to the editorial team at West Virginia University Press for making a home for this essay collection. Thank you to Kristin Link for drawing the map this collection needed.

Thank you to those involved with the "Decolonizing Alaska" exhibit; your work planted the seed that became this book. Thank you to the Yukon Beringia Centre and to Long Ago Yukon, organizations whose programming I attended during my Yukon year and whose speakers, events, and resources influence me still. Thank you also to the Whitehorse Public Library staff who so capably handled my nonstop research requests.

Thank you first to Pepper and then to Rita for your companionship, your unparalleled finesse, and your love. Every word in this book was written alongside one dog or the other.

The bedrock of my thanks goes to my parents, Tam and Greg Cook. You made all of this possible.

NOTES

THE PHOTOGRAPHER (A PRELUDE)

I learned of "semi-abstract landscapes" from the painter Jane Isakson. The photographer—semi-abstracted here as the land is semi-abstracted in Jane's paintings—is digital artist Marten Berkman.

The Little Prince comes from the wartime novella by French writer and aviator: Antoine de Saint-Exupéry, *Le Petit Prince* (1943).

DISTANCE OVER LIGHT

This book, and this essay in particular, is much indebted to William Least Heat-Moon's 1991 book *PrairyErth*. If I've tried to write a deep map of the Alaska-Yukon borderlands, it's thanks to Heat-Moon's discussion of deep mapping and to the poetry he brings to his own deep map of Chase County, Kansas. "Distance Over Light" draws most specifically from *PrairyErth*'s chapter, "Above the Crystalline Basement."

The painter in this essay is Jane Isakson.

SISTER ESSAYS

The Young

Both the US Geologic Survey and the Canada Geologic Survey published terrane maps that this essay reads as works of art.

My thinking in this piece draws from numerous geologic texts but was especially influenced by Yukon University geologist Joel Cubley. He had the generosity to deliver not only one but two personalized lectures to me on the accretionary belt of North America, plate tectonics, and subduction.

How did the world come to be? The quoted summary answering this question comes from Esmé Weijun Wang's 2019 book, *The Collected Schizophrenias*.

The Old

This essay, and my interest in ice patches, was sparked first and foremost by a 2011 booklet put out by the Government of Yukon called *The Frozen Past: The Yukon Ice Patch Project*. The booklet is quite thoughtful in its inclusion of different voices and its comfort in moving between both scientific and spiritual perspectives on ice, artifact, and knowledge.

John Berger's *Ways of Seeing* (1972) is an excellent book for those who try to understand a society by looking at its art. "The Old" dialogues directly with Berger's take on a carved bird; more widely, his *Ways of Seeing* probably influenced my thinking throughout this book.

Phrases including "the contact zone" and "courteous regard" come from Donna Haraway's view of the multi-species, cosmopolitan world and the companion animals we find within it. An especially playful discussion of Haraway's theories appears in her book, *When Species Meet* (2007).

Especially helpful to my project of conjuring past lives on present land was Catharine McClellan's essential 1987 Yukon ethnography, *Part of the Land, Part of the Water: A History of the Yukon Indians* (written with Licie Birckel, Robert Bringhurst, James A. Fall, Carol McCarthy, and Janice R. Sheppard). This work is both ethnography and more than ethnography, as poetry is evident on every page.

I am also eager to point interested readers toward *Kwanlin Dün: Da Kwandur Ghày Ghàkwadîndur—Our Story in Our Words*, a joint project of history, ethnography, photography, and philosophy put together by Kwanlin Dün First Nation and published in 2020.

SWAN SIGNS

I first heard of Doug Smarch Jr.'s feather screen and digital art installation from Valerie Salez, and again, later, from others. Somehow, I understood the screen to be made of white swan feathers, and that is how I've seen it in my head ever since. But when Smarch himself read my essay, he generously offered only one correction: he'd made the screen of turkey feathers. But by then, of course, the artwork's double and doubling histories of Teslin were deeply enmeshed, in my mind, with swans. I must recognize now that this essay sets up the reader to make that same imaginative mistake. My sincere hope is that this causes no harm—and that, rather than standing as an injustice to the history, the misunderstanding opens and infuses it with unexpected life.

Alongside hearsay, conversation, and studying the memories of others, my more formal sources of research on Smarch's digital art installation come from online journalism. For example, *What's Up Yukon* ran a 2013 article on Doug Smarch Jr.'s *Lucinations* that details the fox story, though on my last check, the URL was no longer live. The Kelowna Art Gallery (https://kelownaartgallery.com/2005-2/doug-smarch-jr-lucinations/) and The National Gallery of Canada (https://www.gallery.ca/collection/artwork/lucinations) repeat some of the story.

PERMAFROST IS AN ARCHIVE

Fabrice Calmels, research chair in permafrost and geoscience at the YukonU Research Centre, spearheaded the permafrost field trip I joined in the spring of 2019. On learning that I write about art, Calmels invited me to see the permafrost lab and personally hosted a gregarious (though also quite pensive) lab visit. Later, GIS technician Cyrielle Laurent, also at the YukonU Research Centre, took me on a deep conversational dive into palsa formations.

YFN 101

This essay is built of notes and impressions gathered during my experience of YFN 101. The essay owes its information to my co-teachers and to all who worked to compile the curriculum. Where my notebook was illegible or otherwise incomplete, I roved the Internet to fill in dates, numbers, and names. Errors are my own. With special thanks to Kanina Holmes for involving me in her reconciliation journalism program Stories North and, by extension, in YFN 101.

CHOOUTLA

This essay owes special thanks to former territorial archivist Linda Johnson and to artist Lorraine Wolfe.

This essay begins with an epigraph that is a partial quote from Murray Sinclair, the whole of which is: "Education got us into this mess. Education will get us out." The mess he refers to is, in a word, oppression—something scholarly institutions have actively and implicitly perpetuated for some centuries and, perhaps more recently, attempted to combat. (See Paulo Freire's *Pedagogy of the Oppressed* for a seminal discussion of education's historic use as colonial instrument.) In Sinclair's later years, during a 2023 Q&A with Algonquin College staff and students, he spent some time unpacking the second half of the statement ("education will get us out [of this mess]"). "Education," Sinclair said in that Q&A, "is not about being in school. Education is about learning what it means to be a human being" (https://algonquintimes.com/murray-sinclair-recognizes-the-role-of-education-in-reconciliation/). Sinclair was a former senator, a renowned lawyer, Manitoba's first Indigenous judge, and the former chair of Canada's Truth and Reconciliation Commission.

Another source referenced is Kenneth Coates's article, "'Betwixt and Between': The Anglican Church and the Students of Carcross School." *BC Studies*. Issue No. 64: Winter 1984–85.

Paisley Rekdal's book *Appropriate: A Provocation* (2021) is aptly titled. Yet its central provocation in no way resembles edict or decree. While providing very clear discussion, the book refuses in any way to resolve or simplify appropriation, and for that, it is the sharpest and most important discussion of the issue that I know.

Mapping the Way is a nonpartisan public education initiative created and run by the eleven self-governing Yukon First Nations, the Council of Yukon First Nations, and the governments of Yukon and Canada. Their website is a treasure trove of good history writing. The story "HISTORY OF THE AGREEMENTS: Yukon Association of Non-Status Indians" was of special influence in this essay (https://mappingtheway.ca/stories/yukon-association-non-status-indians).

This essay also draws on historical material published on the Indian Residential School History and Dialogue Centre's website. The IRSHD is a powerhouse of research and public programming at the University of British Columbia (https://irshdc.ubc.ca/learn/indian-residential-schools/).

The Globe and Mail calls itself "a national icon" and "Canada's most recognized media brand." Their staff reporter, Patrick White, wrote a breathtaking piece about Lower Post in 2021 (https://www.theglobeandmail.com/canada/article-lower-post-bc-residential-school/).

GOVERNMENT DOCUMENTS

The artist in this essay is Lianne Charlie. This essay is indebted to her and to the four other artists featured in the Yukon Arts Centre show, "To Talk With Others." Here's what you need to know: The exhibit showcases art responding to the minutes of a 1977 meeting on the then-approved Mackenzie Pipeline. Copies of the minutes were available for viewers to read in the gallery. Those meeting minutes document a formal conversation between then–prime minister Pierre Elliot Trudeau and five Yukon First Nations leaders. The text of their meeting is fascinating: what begins as a discussion about a pipeline becomes a full-blown conversation about First Nations lifeways, autonomy, and self-determination. When artist Valerie Salez found those 1977 meeting minutes in the Tr'ondëk Hwëch'in archives, they gave her the idea for this exhibition—a five-artist show featuring original works by Lianne Charlie, Valerie Salez, Ken Anderson, Doug Smarch Jr., and Joseph Tisiga. Some of the artists spoke with me very briefly, others at length. All five made comments—verbally, yes, but particularly through their artwork—that sparked my thinking in this essay.

Keavy Martin's metaphor of suturing and kinship comes from her book, *Stories in a New Skin: Approaches to Inuit Literature* (2012). This essay also references a line by the surgeon and writer Richard Selzer. For context, please see his essay "The Knife" in *Confessions of a Knife*, 2001.

UNDER THE BRIDGE AT JOHNSON'S CROSSING

This piece comes from a Whitehorse-based arts collaboration called "Circumpolar Duet: Singular Plurality," in which ten word artists and ten visual artists randomly exchanged work. Part I of this essay went to textiles artist Françoise La Roche, who created visual art in dialogue with it. Part II of this essay results from my own dialogue with art I received from ceramicist Astrid Kruse. Haiku poet kjmunro facilitated the collaboration along with with Yukon Writers' Collective Ink and Yukon Artists @ Work.

THE KOHKLUX MAP

This essay is in substantial part the result of dialogue. Special thanks to these interlocutors: Linda Johnson, Tom Buzzell, Frances Woolsey, Ron Chambers, Lani Hotch, Bessie Cooley, Doug Hitch, and Norman Easton.

Our conversations benefited from several exceptionally helpful publications. References to those are: Daniel Henry, *Across the Shaman's River: John Muir, The Tlingit Stronghold, and the Opening of the North*, 2020; Thomas King, *The Inconvenient Indian*, 2013; Kwanlin Dün First Nation, *Kwanlin Dün: Da Kwandur Ghày Ghàkwadîndur—Our Story in Our Words*, 2020; and Yukon Historical and Museums Association, *The Kohklux Map*, 1995.

"Our Trails Bring Us Together," the October 2019 Kohklux Map conference, fed my thinking tremendously. Some of the more tangible resources from the conference include talks, specifically these two: Norman Easton's talk, "Anthropology and the Construction of Geophysical Cultural Boundaries in the Western Subarctic of North America," and Deborah Kent's talk, "Glorious Beyond Description: A Solar Eclipse for American Science, 1869." Also of exceptional service to my learning and fact-checking were the nine final conference panels/banners. They were written cooperatively by project partners Yukon Historical and Museums Association (YHMA), Kwanlin Dün Cultural Centre, and Jilk̲aat K̲wáan Heritage Center.

THE ASH AND THE LITERATURE

I've cited and dialogued with a variety of sources in this essay, which include Anne Bradstreet's "For My Dear Son Simon Bradstreet" (1630)—the version I used was anthologized in *The Making of the American Essay*, edited by John

D'Agata (2016)—Francisco Cantú, *The Line Becomes a River: Dispatches from the Border* (2018); two works by Todd J. Kristensen, "Fingerprints in Glass: Obsidian and Ancient Human Relationships," from *RETROactive: Exploring Alberta's Past* (Government of Alberta, 2021), and "Power, security, and exchange: Impacts of a Late Holocene volcanic eruption in Subarctic North America," in *North American Archaeologist* (2021); "History, Science, and the 'Year of Two Winters': Uncovering the Secrets of Dene Migration," by Walter Strong, with input from John Ives and Todd Kristensen (CBC North, 2017); and Thomas, Christian, et al.'s "Yukon First Nation Use of Copper for End-Blades on Hunting Arrows," in *Journal of Glacial Archaeology* (2017).

And while my essay omits direct mention of Kathryn Nuernberger's essay collection, *The Witch of Eye* (2021), I found it haunting—and therefore quite relevant—to my work here. Most explicitly, my essay borrows and repeats the comparison that Nuernberger makes between June 2019 and 1879–1918. In other words, it's Nuernberger who points out that the 13,000 children apprehended recently at the US border numerically resemble the 12,000 children placed in the infamous Carlisle Indian School.

A TRIANGLE OF SUN

This essay comes from a day in the field at the Bonanza Research Station near Fairbanks, Alaska. I went there as an artist with the University of Alaska Fairbanks NEH-funded arts-and-science collaboration, "In a Time of Change" (ITOC). ITOC has been running for several years now; my experience was with its 2020–2022 "Boreal Forest Stories" cohort. At one point, I had an hour to teach creative writing to some of my fellow collaborators—among others, we were poets, ceramicists, painters, filmmakers, botanists, ecologists, microbiologists . . . I led a metaphor-making exercise called "Fact, Fact, Image." At the end, I invited volunteers to rip out and donate their notebook pages to me for a collage essay. Several were so generous as to do so. Therefore, this piece owes special thanks to the fearless Boreal Forest Stories ITOC participants whose pages came home with me: Kelsey Aho, Susan Grace, Margo Klass, Mary Beth Leigh, Dana Lindauer, Debbie Moderow, Jen Moss, Oralee Nudson, Jeremy Pataky, Teresa Shannon, and Molissa Udevitz. Their language appears throughout this essay.

So do words and ideas gleaned from three sources in particular. First and foremost, I recognize much of this life's strangeness in the tiny, reverie-soaked essayistic gem by young Barry Lopez, *Desert Notes / River Notes* (1976). Alongside this debt to Barry Lopez, I also drew heavily from anthropology writings by Lewis Hyde (*Trickster Makes this World: Mischief, Myth, and Art*, 1998) and by Tom Thornton and Yadvinder Malhi ("The Trickster in the Anthropocene," *The Anthropocene Review*, 2016).

THE END

"The future blows like a wind through the streets . . ." Yes: that precise wind blows through the streets of Rebecca Solnit's *Infinite City: A San Francisco Atlas* (2010) as well as it blows through northern forests peopled by the family, neighbors, and artists of this book.

Photo credit: Carl Brodersen

Corinna Cook is the author of the essay collection *Leavetakings*. Her writing appears in *Ploughshares, Alaska Quarterly Review, Assay: A Journal of Nonfiction Studies*, and elsewhere. A former Fulbright Fellow, Cook's writing has also received support from the National Endowment for the Humanities, the Rasmuson Foundation, the Alaska State Council on the Arts, and an Alaska Literary Award. She is a graduate of Pomona College and holds a PhD in English and creative writing from the University of Missouri. Cook teaches nonfiction in Alaska Pacific University's low-residency MFA program in creative writing and lives in Juneau, Alaska.